FROM MY LEVEL

Frontispiece   *From a drawing by Youngman Carter*

GEORGE MALLABY

—— ★ ——

FROM MY LEVEL

ATHENEUM   NEW YORK

1965

To my wife

Contents

——— ★ ———

Preface

—— ★ ——

My life has been most fortunate and my experiences most varied. Some of this I have wanted to share with my readers— not the plans and the policies and the secrets of our fevered years, but the attitudes and manners and personalities of some of our chief of men and of our military leaders. I am indebted to no documents and no diaries. I have drawn only upon deep and lasting impressions and sensitive memories. My contemporaries, my friends, those *on* my level, will, I hope, find the book readable and entertaining. It will remind them of much hard toil and much fun and friendship which we shared together. For men in the generations after mine, many of whom already think of the last war in terms of impersonal history, the book is intended to provide warm and living pictures of some of the great characters of our age. Great happiness and rich sympathies spring from a sense of kinship with the past. To young men, still at universities and still reviewing the careers open to them, I hope the book will be strong evidence of the attractions, in interest, in excitement and in colour, of a life in the public service.

The object and the method of the book decided for me the form of the index. This is no more than a list of the names of the men and women who figure in its pages. In writing of them I have used the form of name and title which seemed to me to suit my context, but in the index they are shown under their present style and title or their style and title at death.

I acknowledge with thanks the permission given me by the Countess Wavell, on behalf of the executors of the first Earl Wavell, and by Messrs. Collins, to print *in extenso* the letter on pages 94–6.

I am especially grateful to Miss Mary Forth, who has found time in a very busy life to help me most unselfishly in the production of this book, and to my publisher for his most generous confidence.

G.M.

Foreword

Levels

Levels are very significant in all walks of life in this country. Society, for all the efforts of radicals and levellers, continues to be constructed on different levels. There may be less privilege, less patronage for those born on elevated levels, and more opportunities, more consideration, more assistance for those born on lower levels. It is easier, that is to say, to advance from a low level to a higher one, and to descend from inherited grandeur to a level of neglect and mediocrity. It, nevertheless, remains true that in society different levels do not regularly commingle. Dukes and dustmen do not dine together. This, we are told by the reformers and the disaffected, is because our country is, and always has been, class-ridden; that may be so, but I have not myself observed any difference in this regard in any of the up-to-date egalitarian democracies of the world, not in the U.S.A., not even in New Zealand, and certainly, I am told, not in the Soviet Union. People of similar education and interests are naturally drawn to each other and there is nothing very wrong about that.

Apart from society, the work of the country is organised on different levels. The farmer has agricultural workers who do his bidding, industry is a series of levels from bench to board, headmasters give orders to assistant masters, bishops are superior to curates, judges are rude to Q.C.s. Nowhere are the levels more obviously defined than in the service of government. The Civil Service itself is, in the main, organised on three levels: the Administrative Class, the Executive Class and the Clerical Class, and their equivalents in the Scientific and Professional Civil Services; the Fighting Services also on three: the officers, the N.C.O.s and the other ranks. But the top level of the Civil Service and the Fighting Services is quite a different level from the level of Ministers of the Crown. For very good reasons there is a great gulf fixed at that point and I thought that the title of my book would be more significant and the incidents in it easier to follow if I made some brief explanation here.

Everybody knows about politicians, everybody knows the faces and the mannerisms and the attitudes of Ministers and prominent members of the Opposition. When things go well, when there is reasonable peace and contentment and affluence, the Government, that is to say Ministers, get praise and applause. When things go badly they are vilified and abused and the leaders of the Opposition take on a more attractive look. This is as it should be. Ministers are responsible for governing the country. They make the decisions that lead to success or adversity. They deserve the praise and must endure the blame. That is accepted and understood, but what is not understood is how they reach the decisions which they make. How can a bunch of politicians come to decide that we ought to build so many houses a year, that we ought to accept the offer of Polaris submarines, that we ought to nationalise the steel industry—or that we ought to de-nationalise it—that we should subsidise farmers in certain well-defined directions, or put duties on this or taxes on that, or send a definite number of troops to Cyprus and so on? How can twenty or so politicians sitting round a table at No. 10 Downing Street reach decisions on such diverse matters, each one probably impinging on another and all putting a burden of some kind on the national economy? And when they have reached their decisions how on earth do they carry them out? The answer, of course, is that the Government, whatever its colour, has permanent advisers. The advisers are the Civil Service and the Fighting Services. They work out the problems—the cost of building so many houses a year, the burden on the economy of agricultural subsidies, the strategic value of Polaris submarines, the value and the cost of sending troops to Cyprus and so on. They give the facts and they offer advice based on the facts and Ministers decide. When Ministers have decided it is the civil servants who give effect to their decisions.

It follows, then, that the top civil servants, the so-called Permanent Secretaries of the great Departments of State, the Treasury, the Foreign Office, the Board of Trade, the Ministry of Agriculture, the Ministry of Transport, and all the rest, and the heads of the Fighting Services, the Chief of the Defence Staff, the First Sea Lord (now the Chief of the Naval Staff), the Chief of the Imperial General Staff (now the Chief of the General Staff), the Chief of the Air Staff, are very close to Ministers, always at their side, ready with help and advice and ready to carry out the Ministers' decisions when they have reached them. The ultimate responsibility, as I have said, is the Minister's and he should have the limelight. That is why so little is known of top civil servants and even in' the Fighting Services—especially in war—the great Commanders-in-Chief in the field are much better known to the public than the Chiefs of Staff, the close advisers of the Government. That is why civil servants are so careful not to infringe the line of demarcation between their level and the level of their political masters.

I had myself come from altogether different circumstances. I was well accustomed to the levels of scholastic life, since I had passed my first fifteen working years in the profession of a schoolmaster. Discipline, obedience, conformity are built into the structure of public schools, and although there is a certain egalitarian freemasonry between assistant masters of every age and standing, there is between assistant masters and headmaster a wide area for obsequious attentions (or dumb insolence) on the one side and for *ex-cathedra* pronouncements and direct orders on the other. Furthermore, there is a zone of almost complete silence between assistant masters and governors. In general I was fortunate because for ten of the eleven years which I spent at St. Edward's School, Oxford, Henry Kendall had been my chief. This friendly man could dominate and direct but he could not be remote and he could not be pompous. He loved his fellow men. When I myself became Headmaster of St. Bees I tried in a rather difficult three years to follow his example. It was by no means easy, I found, to leave one's level and to mix with levels below. Headmasters are autocrats—they have more unfettered power than any other class of people in any profession—and the benevolence of autocrats is never taken on trust. When I moved away from this world and took on, in faith and hope, the job of District Commissioner for the Special Area of West Cumberland I was soon made aware that away in London there was a level above me. I was a government official, a temporary civil servant; my job was to do what I could with somewhat limited powers to help to attract new industries to this area of long-sustained and tragic unemployment, running at that time at about thirty-five per cent of the insured popula-tion. One of the factors which limited the appeal of West Cumberland to industrialists was the lack of road and rail facilities. In public speeches I exhorted the people of West Cumberland to shout and shout again and to keep on shouting until the Government gave them a West Coast road. I was very soon reminded in sharp terms by the level above me, the Special Areas Commissioner himself and his headquarters staff in London, that I was myself a servant of the Government and that it ill became me to preach sedition against it. I was no longer the autocrat of St. Bees.

When the war came man-power became a priceless asset and unemployment was cured in a day. I had a commission in the Emergency Reserve and after a restless and frustrating period in the office of the Regional Transport Commissioner in Manchester (where it seemed that I was deliberately kept below the working level) I was called up and commissioned on the General List. It is at this point that the experiences which I have recounted in this book make their beginning and they continue into post-war times when I became an established civil servant. During all these experiences I was not on the top level of civil servants and nowhere near the top level of soldiers during the war. But I was on a convenient level for observation. I was not the confidant of Ministers, but I was near enough to them to observe their manners and attitudes. Although in the war I held only lowly rank, I was centrally placed and able to observe at close quarters some of the great war leaders. This intermediate sort of position—a second-level civil servant and a low-level soldier in a main-line station—not only enabled me to observe but has left me free to comment without any breach of confidence. I have moreover refrained throughout from commenting on the substance of policies. Indeed I have hardly mentioned policies. Deeply involved as I have been in many political and strategic problems, it is far from my purpose in this book to probe and explore these and to claim, as many authors seem to do, that the most successful solutions were those advocated by me. My book is about men, the men who argued about these problems, decided them and gave the orders. My interest is in the personalities, the attitudes, the mannerisms, the style of these men.

Much of what I have written about Sir Winston Churchill and Earl Attlee is derived from my contacts with them when they were Prime Ministers and I was what is known as an

Under-Secretary (roughly the Civil Service equivalent of a Major-General) in the Cabinet Office. The duty of the civil servants in the Cabinet Office is to serve the Cabinet itself and all its various committees, some composed of Ministers, some of officials, some of both. 'Serving' the Cabinet and its committees means something rather special on which I might perhaps say a word. It must be fairly widely known that meetings of men or women, whether they are called committees or working parties or anything else, are confused and indecisive unless they are presided over by a strong chairman and served by a strong secretariat. The Cabinet and its committees are no exception. A heavy responsibility falls upon the civil servants in the Cabinet Office—the Cabinet Secretariat—to make sure that the necessary papers are prepared and circulated, the Agenda drawn up, the meeting properly convened, the chairman fully and clearly briefed on points of procedure, the decisions, with supporting arguments, precisely recorded and action initiated accordingly. There are somewhat stylised techniques about some of this, invented and developed by the three Secretaries of the Cabinet since the start of a Cabinet Secretariat in 1916—the late Lord Hankey, Lord Bridges and Lord Normanbrook—and there is no doubt that the processes of the Cabinet Office have contributed indispensable articulation to the machinery of government. In this book I have tried to get away from these techniques. I am not here concerned with the articulation of the machinery of government. I am concerned with men and not with organisations.

I well remember on a certain morning sometime in 1953, while Brook and I were standing outside the Cabinet room at No. 10 waiting, along with Ministers, to be summoned inside by the Prime Minister for a Cabinet meeting, we were approached by Harold Macmillan, at that time Minister of Housing. 'You know, you fellows' he said, 'are falsifying history.' Pointing to his copy of the minutes of the last Cabinet meeting

he went on: 'Look at this! Historians reading this fifty or a
hundred years hence will get a totally false picture. They will
be filled with admiration and surprise to find that the Cabinet
were so intellectually disciplined that they argued each issue
methodically and logically through to a set of neat and precise
conclusions. It isn't like that at all and you know it.' We did
know it, only too well, but the form of minutes preferred by
Brook, and perfected by him, was the best way of getting
action taken, getting something done as a result of all the
argument and discussion. Since I was trained in these ways, all
the meetings, civil or military, which I have attended as
Secretary have been rounded off in the same way and action
initiated accordingly. The events which followed, the consequences of these decisions, are a part of history and in this
book it is not about them I wish to write. In this book I have
thrown aside my training and instead of writing minutes of
meetings in approved Cabinet Office style I have tried to
reproduce something of the atmosphere and colour, odd
memories of chance remarks, stormy passages, individual
appearances and attitudes—all the things in fact which, in the
correct severity of our training, we were expressly enjoined to
exclude from our minutes.

My recollections of Mr. Macmillan and of New Zealand
Prime Ministers are based on a rather different level of experience. Nearly all of them are derived from my time in New
Zealand, where I was, from April 1957 to August 1959, the
British High Commissioner. A High Commissioner's relationship with the Prime Minister of the country to which he is
accredited and with his own Prime Minister is totally different
from the relationship of an Under-Secretary in the Cabinet
Office with the Prime Minister of this country. A High
Commissioner represents his Government in a Commonwealth
country. He speaks to the Prime Minister of that Commonwealth country in the person of the United Kingdom Prime

B

Minister. By virtue of his office, therefore, he moves upon a
higher level and in my relations with New Zealand Prime
Ministers I could, if occasion demanded, behave to them with a
confident hauteur which a civil servant in this country would
never assume. There were in fact few occasions which called
for frigid attitudes. All three New Zealand Prime Ministers
whom I knew were straightforward friendly men and we lived
on terms of equality and friendship. My contacts with my own
Prime Minister, Mr. Macmillan, during this time would
normally have been at the end of a wire and even that would
have come into play only when matters were of such importance that they required personal messages between Mr.
Macmillan and the New Zealand Prime Minister. A good many
such messages, I am glad to say, are deemed necessary and useful and this direct personal link between Prime Ministers of the
Commonwealth is one of the most distinguishing features of
the Commonwealth system. When a Prime Minister tells the
House of Commons that he is consulting his Commonwealth
colleagues he means that he is sending personal messages
through the United Kingdom High Commissioners who are
delivering them to the other Commonwealth Prime Ministers,
discussing them with them and sending back their replies,
together with any gloss or comment which the High Commissioners think it useful to add. It so happened that when I was
in New Zealand Mr. Macmillan paid that country an eight-day
visit and, in accordance with normal practice, I, as High
Commissioner, was in attendance on him throughout. My duty
during this time was to explain local problems, interpret New
Zealand personalities and in general to do my best to be a useful
travelling companion.

   In Chapters 2 and 3 I am but a minion to the Gods of War,
both at home and at their war-time conferences, but, as I have
said before, within clear earshot of some of them. From
December 1940 till June 1942 I was a General Staff officer in a

section of the War Office named Military Operations 5 (M.O.5). It would be inappropriate here to try to describe the complex and multifarious duties of the Military Operations Directorate of the War Office, especially in war-time. It is perhaps enough to say that I was a cog in the machine part of whose duty it was to keep the C.I.G.S. fully informed of the actual facts of operations in progress all over the world, of the consequences, in terms of man-power and material, of these operations, their likely result and their effect upon other operations either in progress or in prospect—in other words to give the C.I.G.S. the bricks with which he and the other Chiefs of Staff and the Prime Minister might construct a strategy of the war. Our prime duty was to look at these problems from the Army point of view, though we should have been purblind if we had not seen and tried to understand the problems of the other two Services and the often overriding political consider-ations. There was, however, an inter-Service staff, known as the Joint Planning Staff, whose prime duty it was to look at these problems from the point of view of all three Services and also of the Foreign Service. To this Joint Planning Staff I was transferred in June 1942.

The Joint Planning Staff was composed of officers drawn from all three Services, together with a representative of the Foreign Office and advisers from the Ministry of Transport, the Ministry of Economic Warfare and other authorities as required. We worked in teams of three in a part of the offices of the War Cabinet. We did our examinations and made our reports to the three Directors of Plans (a Captain R.N., a Brigadier and an Air Commodore), who then submitted reports direct to the Committee of the Chiefs of Staff (the C.I.G.S., the C.A.S. and the First Sea Lord). The whole of this staff was served by a secretariat, two or three serving officers who themselves were members of the Military Secretariat of the War Cabinet headed by General Lord Ismay. After a year

as a member of one of the teams I was made the Secretary of
the Joint Planning Staff and this I remained for the rest of the
war. Most of my recollections are drawn from this time. In this
capacity I attended the war-time conferences which I have
attempted to describe in Chapter 3. In this capacity I attended,
over a period of a year or so, the daily meetings of the Chiefs of
Staff with, as it were, a watching brief for the Directors of
Plans. I attempted as a result to interpret to the Chiefs of Staff
what the Joint Planning Staff thought about certain strategic
problems and to explain to the Joint Planning Staff precisely
what further examinations were needed and how they might
most profitably be carried out. I was what might be described
as 'a low-level link' between the Chiefs of Staff Committee and
the Joint Planning Staff. From that level a man can see and learn
much and it was in the Joint Planning Staff, through arduous
days and nights of hard argument and long intellectual grind,
that I discovered the strength and influence to be derived from
listening, listening with fixed and concentrated attention. It is no
part of a Secretary's job to enter the argument or maintain his
own point of view, however much he may want to, however
trivial and irritating he may find the arguments of others. At
the end of the day, when all are exhausted by their efforts to
make their own arguments prevail and have retired to their
own tents to lick their wounds, the Secretary alone possesses
the field. He must now make a synthesis of the opinions hurled
violently in all directions throughout the contest, he must make
a synthesis, but it must be positive, brief and constructive. This
calls for some special skills of mind and temperament, skills
which by patience, concentration and silence can be acquired.
In later years when I worked closely with the French they were
inclined to respect and admire this expertise of a British
Secretary. '*La synthèse*,' General Ely used to say to me. '*La
synthèse—c'est le travail d'un cerveau*'—and he was quite
right; and he might have added that the one brain must

belong to a man who is able to keep himself emotionally insulated.

I have included a chapter on meetings of Commonwealth Prime Ministers because in a rapidly changing Commonwealth scene there may be some faint historical interest in a picture of what they were like twelve or fifteen years ago.

In Chapter 5 I deal at some length with the work of the Brussels Treaty Defence Organization. The Brussels Treaty was the beginning of attempts to achieve some effective unity in Western Europe and led directly to the vaster and more comprehensive alliance, the North Atlantic Treaty. It has therefore a historic importance and its early struggles for unity and coherence are interesting in themselves and because they brought into close co-operation or conflict certain personalities of great significance. My part in all this was once again the part of a Secretary, but this time I was an international Secretary and not a British one only. I served—impartially as I thought—the Committee of the Ministers of Defence of the Five Signatory Powers (Great Britain, France, the Netherlands, Belgium and Luxembourg), the Committee of the Chiefs of Staff of these Five Powers and a military committee of permanent representatives of the Five Powers at Major-General level meeting regularly in London. I look back on this period—not untroubled, as the reader will see—as one of the happiest and most constructive periods in my life.

These, then, were the levels from which I watched my notable actors. Sometimes they were a long way above me, but in good perspective, all the same. At other times my level was a little nearer to theirs, but it was never the same. This book is not about those on my level, my own friends—though some make occasional but incidental appearances because they are essential to the particular scene I am trying to describe or to the effect I am trying to produce.

I added a sub-titled 'Unwritten Minutes' which, though not equally applicable to all chapters, puts briefly the general form of the book—the attempt to let life and colour into official occasions, and to show that the brief and frigid phrases of official pronouncements often conceal a wealth of human activity and the continuous exercise and interplay of living personalities.

I

Our Chief of Men

PRIME MINISTERS seemed to me in the years before the war to be figures so elevated and so remote that I was no more likely to encounter them in my lifetime than to fly the Atlantic. Yet if flying the Atlantic and meeting Prime Ministers are worth-while objectives I have accomplished both several times over. Nearly everyone by now has flown the Atlantic and there is really nothing much to say about it. Prime Ministers are a different matter. Until the war my awareness of them was from the newspapers, from listening occasionally to their political speeches, and from gossiping with people who, I fondly thought, knew them at first hand and told bold stories of what the P.M. said; even the use of the initial letters seemed to me, in my green years, to be evidence of a close and exciting familiarity. Suddenly these distant beings assumed a greater and warmer proximity when my brother told me that not infrequently on his daily way to the War Office he met Neville Chamberlain taking a solitary walk in St. James's Park and that this woebegone figure acknowledged the raising of my brother's hat with a melancholy and wintry smile. After all, Prime Ministers were made of flesh and blood, could be seen walking in the park, and would return the courtesy of an ordinary man.

So far as I remember I never even saw Neville Chamberlain. I had little wish to. I shared with most of my countrymen the sense of relief which the shameful settlement at Munich brought but I had no illusions, and, as the news came through and as Mr. Chamberlain seemed genuinely proud of his paltry piece of paper and confident of its validity, I took myself for a solitary walk along the slopes above Crummock Water lost in miserable doubts and speculations. Even the rape of Czechoslovakia failed to shake the impenetrable self-confidence of that dreary man. His policy was in shreds. He had clearly lost his game, but no resignation came. He still felt that he alone could guide and lead us, he, the obstinate, blind, misguided man, who in the range of international affairs had missed the target every time. I was the man in the street in those days; I had no inside information of any kind. My judgments were formed by reading newspapers and periodicals; by occasional conversations with the Bishop of Carlisle, Dr. Williams, a wise old man who had the ear of the Archbishop and knew a thing or two; by a chance meeting in a Lakeland hotel with C. F. Allen, sensitive, sincere, intelligent, who talked freely with me; by the daily outpourings of Jack Adams, exaggerated and extravagant sometimes, but penetrating, lively, sharp; by an occasional visit to London and a word or two with my brother, most of whose information was Top Secret and not for my ears.

When the inevitable happened and war came I listened with a sinking heart to the Prime Minister's thin, self-pitying, plaintive tones as he announced that we were at war with Germany. We needed to be braced to battle, a clarion call, a summons to our courage and our tenacity. We received the feeble apologetics of a failure. Not too soon this nerveless dying man gave place to the one man who could rouse us and save us. At the last hour he came to us, but it was time enough for his genius.

Sir Winston Churchill

So much has been written and spoken about Sir Winston Churchill—some of it so well said—that it is difficult to say anything fresh and rather easy to become a bore. Stories about him, his habits, his sayings, abound and at one time were the common currency of conversation. There were many unscrupulous inventions, generally detectable by those who had known the man at first hand and were well aware of the authentic style. Like Dr. Johnson he is almost inimitable, and indeed the sayings of both are so witty and often so wise that there is no need to go outside the accepted canon and attempt pinchbeck imitations. If Sir Winston had his Boswell he must have worked silently and unseen. There would have been even less toleration of a man with a notebook sitting behind him at meals and a violent and immediate snub for anyone who attempted to lead him into conversation by infantile and provocative questions. And yet—what a subject for a Boswell! What a chance missed!

I did for a year or two, while taking notes at Cabinet meetings, include in my notes the more striking phrases of the Prime Minister, an occasional anecdote perhaps, from time to time a reproach to one of his colleagues in subtle terms or some phrase of seduction spoken wooingly to another colleague whose wavering opinion he hoped to win over to his own, some wise opinions on the conduct of politicians, allusive echoes and boyish teasing nonsense. I wrote them down and some have stayed in my mind, but my notebooks, crammed full of secrets and confidences, all went to destruction in what is known as secret waste.

At my first encounter with this extraordinary man he was invisible to me—a voice over the telephone lisping out blurred

and difficult questions to my trembling ears. I was on night
duty in the War Office in early 1941 I think—answering as best
I could for the whole of my section (M.O.5), which handled
operations in the Middle East Command. My own particular
tasks were Greece and Crete and Syria, but at night everything
else came upon one—usually perhaps not much more than
marking the distributions on telegrams (a complicated business)
or writing up situation reports, sometimes outrageous crisis and
emergency when others more senior and more skilful had to be
summoned from their beds and the whole dreadful machine
was got in motion. This night I was sitting half dressed hard at
my routine stuff in our night duty room somewhere in the
basement, files and papers and telegrams and maps hemming
me in, telephones ringing every few minutes and my poor G.I.,
Lieutenant-Colonel W. S. Cole, trying to get some sleep on an
uncomfortable bunk in the corner. The telephone rang again
and with a muttered curse I snatched it up. 'M.O.5,' I said
briskly, and a voice replied, 'The Prime Minister wishes to
speak to you.' At first I thought it was a leg-pull by an idle
night duty officer in some other section. The Prime Minister
had never been known to speak direct to a section. It was
unheard of. His contacts were with the C.I.G.S., and D.M.O.
at the very lowest. 'Come off it,' I was about to remark into the
telephone when the well-known voice began. This was no
imitation. He wanted to know a lot of things about the
campaign in Abyssinia and Eritrea—things remote from my
knowledge and experience, as far from my particular responsibilities as they could be. I played it carefully, watching the ball
with eagle eyes, forward defensive prods for the most part, but
occasionally a more daring stroke was needed. 'What is the
distance from Harar to Addis Ababa?' the voice somewhat
peremptorily enquired. An answer had to be given. I had no
idea. I had hardly heard of Harar. I cast an agonised glance at
an outline map not drawn to scale in the litter around me and

made a wild calculation from it. Boldly I named a figure, the
sweat pouring down my face. Surely my bluff was called, but
there was no adverse reaction. By this time Colonel Cole was
awake and aware that I was engaged in a direct conversation
with the Prime Minister on a subject of which I knew nothing.
In great agitation he was revolving at speed around my table,
longing to snatch the instrument from my hand and rescue the
reputation of M.O.5. But I could not let go. At the Prime
Minister's end there was no intermission, 'no mitigation or
remorse of voice', and at our end we could not change voices in
midstream; that would have aroused his suspicions at once. I
had to play out time and fortunately for us he was amiable and
good-humoured, seeming to enjoy the conversation and quite
unaware of the panic in my heart and of the frustrated excitement of my G.I. At last he said 'Good night' in friendly tones.
No harm was done and indeed this performance was repeated
on many occasions. It pleased him to speak direct to an officer
of lowly rank who was right in the middle of the job. He was
not always equally amiable and sometimes we were held
personally responsible for what he thought were the mistakes
and failures of General Wavell and other commanders.

My last encounter was in some ways rather more alarming.
In 1954 I was leaving the Cabinet Office after three years of
fairly close though impersonal contact with the Prime Minister
to go and do a job in Kenya. Sir Norman Brook had obtained
the Prime Minister's written agreement to my departure. All
arrangements had been made, air passages booked, inoculations
administered, tropical kit purchased and so on. The Secretary
of State, then Oliver Lyttelton, had notified the Government of
Kenya, who were anxious that I should hurry up and get on
with the job. Brook asked the Prime Minister if he would say
goodbye to me after a Cabinet meeting on the following day
and he assented. Accordingly we waited in the Cabinet room
after Ministers had departed and it was only then that the

Prime Minister connected my name with my face. Certainly he had agreed to 'Mallaby' going to Kenya, but nobody had told him who 'Mallaby' was. Turning upon Brook he said: 'Why have you organised this? I could not possibly agree that he should leave us and go to Kenya. He has been with us all the time. He knows all our secrets. He is much more useful here than he would be there. Somebody else must be found to go to Kenya. We cannot have new people, raw and inexperienced, coming in and meddling with these grave questions which confront us. No, I could not possibly agree.' This was most disturbing, but Brook, as usual, was quite equal to the moment and began to explain patiently that all had been arranged and that it was not possible to disappoint the Secretary of State and the Government of Kenya at this last moment. The Prime Minister was not pleased, sat brooding and then turned upon me. 'Do you want to go?' he asked. In my secret heart at that time I did not want to go. I was dreading the whole thing. Here was the opportunity to get out of it, but ruefully I pushed the cheap temptation aside and made myself utter the stock reply of duty, 'Naturally I will go wherever I am sent.' 'Of course you would say that!' he retorted, and turned again upon Brook. What had I done wrong? Why did Brook wish to get rid of me? It was not wise to make all these unnecessary changes amongst persons placed in positions of special confidence. Patiently Brook took up the tale again. I had done a stretch of four years in the Cabinet Office, longer than was customary. I should have to move on soon, in any case, and it so happened that Kenya were in particular need of someone with my experience. The Prime Minister listened gloomily and an uncomfortable silence supervened. Then suddenly and without further question or argument he turned to me and said, 'Well, it only remains for me to say goodbye and wish you the best of luck,' and he held out his pink delicate hand and gave me a most friendly smile.

Thirteen years separated these two encounters. For six of these Sir Winston was in opposition and I saw nothing of him. My official contacts were with Mr. Attlee. But during the other seven I was close enough to him to feel at first hand the force of his personality, to observe the deployment of his powers, to note some of his idiosyncrasies, to fear his rage, to marvel at his compassion, to laugh at his boyish spirits and to respect his occasional weakness. He was sixty-six when he alarmed my ignorance on the telephone and seventy-nine when he persuaded himself against his nature to give me a friendly goodbye. These are not commonly thought to be the most vigorous or most constructive years of a man's life. Many men never attain them at all and when they do their life is often but labour and sorrow. Sir Winston was at his peak almost continuously throughout them. He had illnesses—serious illnesses—but the enforced rest which they imposed served to increase his vigour, and apart from a slight hardness of hearing —sometimes diplomatic—there was very little diminution of power at the end of this period.

His appearance was always a surprise. It was not only that he liked gaudy dressing-gowns, odd hats and rompers. In fact for most of the time he dressed conventionally, short black coat, striped trousers, a blue bow tie with white spots and impeccably clean linen; and on that score he would hardly have been noticed in a crowd of Londoners. What he said and wrote and all that was told about him led one to expect a more violent, more masculine-looking man, rough and rugged like Cromwell or proud and remote like the younger Pitt. He was nothing of the kind. He was short, delicate-looking, pink and white, round-faced, had wispy hair, frail artistic hands. He stumped along rather than walked, but when he sat, he sat heavily, broodingly, like a man six feet tall and twenty stone, mono-lithic in his chair. Then when the discussions began that child-like face became the reflection of the man—the set bulldog look, so well known in his photographs and portraits, the sulky look of a pouting child, the angry violent look of an animal at bay, the tearful look of a compassionate woman and the sudden spontaneous smiling look of a boy. The moods changed rapidly. Sometimes the sulk and the pout seemed to have set in with little hope of a thaw, but it was not so, and humour generally came to the rescue earlier than anyone expected. Not always so: there were times in the war, as readers of Lord Alanbrooke's diaries will know, when critical opposition was carried beyond the limit of obstinacy and the fight was conducted with any weapon that lay to hand. Defeat was never admitted, apologies were never made. Acquiescence, when it was finally given on one point, was immediately followed by blasts of invective on another. Very often there was a scene, always a performance by the Prime Minister. It was never a humdrum routine meeting speedily and decisively completed. I am speaking of official meetings only. I had no opportunities to observe the Prime Minister in other circumstances. When he came back to power at the end of 1951 his powers of aggression were undiminished, but perhaps he employed them a little less. I do not think it could be said, however, that he mellowed with old age. Mellow is the last adjective to describe him. He remained sharp and vigorous and alarming; only his powers of endurance were somewhat abated.

Anybody who served anywhere near him was devoted to him. It is hard to say why. He was not kind or considerate. He bothered nothing about us. He knew the names only of those very close to him and would hardly let anyone else come into his presence. He was free with abuse and complaint. He was exacting beyond reason and ruthlessly critical. He continuously exhibited all the characteristics which one usually deplores and abominates in the boss. Not only did he get away with it but nobody really wanted him otherwise. He was unusual, unpredictable, exciting, original, stimulating, provocative, outrageous, uniquely experienced, abundantly talented, humorous, entertaining—almost everything a man could be, a great man.

To me the endearing thing was the boyish sense of fun, the natural unpremeditated humour, the sudden smile at some private thought. I remember my brother telling me about a meeting with the Prime Minister in 1941 at which he accompanied the C.I.G.S. and other high-ranking officers from the three Services. They were discussing the situation in Iraq, Rashid Ali's rebellion, the threat to our oil supplies, etc. It was a serious, anxious discussion and the Prime Minister, as usual, was angry at the cautious attitude of his military advisers. And yet in the midst of his anger his imagination was caught up by the Iraqi place names—in particular Bakuba—and from his startled and for the most part uncomprehending audience he suddenly demanded, 'What's Bakuba to him or he to Bakuba?'

There are other well-authenticated stories of the same kind. A distinguished economist was introduced into a Committee of Ministers during the war to explain the paramount importance of buffer stocks. This was not the sort of subject likely to make an immediate appeal to the Prime Minister's attention and in any case he very much resented the intrusion of strange faces into these secret and confidential conclaves. He bore the explanation with mounting intolerance. Then turning to Sir Edward Bridges, sitting next to him, he enquired in a loud voice, 'What is he talking about?' 'He is explaining about buffer stocks,' said Bridges. 'About what?' 'About buffer stocks,' said Bridges in a louder voice. 'Oh,' said the Prime Minister, 'I thought you said butter scotch.' This very characteristic sally had a double purpose. It was funny in itself—a funny connection of sounds as in the Bakuba story—and it served to deflate the economist whose easy command of his subject irritated the Prime Minister. Unless you are yourself the victim of this sort of thing it is difficult not to be amused and seduced by it. A very composed and melancholy military man, unassuming, unsmiling, cadaverous, was once representing his Service, in the absence of his chief, at a meeting with the Prime Minister. The Prime Minister, irritated, very likely, by the absence of the chief, delivered an unexpected and grossly unfair attack upon some action taken or neglected by that Service. To this the cadaverous one, in even, unemotional tones, returned a logical and wholly convincing reply. Momentarily the Prime Minister was silenced, but he soon had his revenge. 'Who is that?' he loudly enquired of General Ismay. General Ismay gave him the name and rank of this skeleton intruder and after a minute's reflection the Prime Minister observed in ringing tones, 'He looks pretty cocky, doesn't he?' In their own style these escapes from defeat are comparable with Johnson's retort to the perfectly sober man who over dinner was clearly winning an argument about the passions—'There is one passion,' Dr. Johnson roared, 'which I advise you to beware of. When you have finished that glass, don't take another.'

It was during the war years that I first attended a meeting presided over by the Prime Minister. It was one of those late-night affairs which burnt into Lord Alanbrooke's memory—a meeting between him and the Chiefs of Staff, with Mr. Eden thrown in to add to the political weight. General Ismay, of course, was in attendance, and General Hollis and I were there to keep the record and see that the decisions were at once put into operation. General Hollis warned me clearly that I might not survive the first few minutes, that I might be at once ejected as an unnecessary stranger and that at best I should be subjected to a baleful and suspicious stare. I managed to survive, but there was no doubt about the stare and if the Prime Minister's attention had not been suddenly distracted I think he was about to ask me my name—which in the circumstances I should have been quite unable to remember. The meeting was not so uncomfortable and stormy as we had expected. Everyone was tired except the Prime Minister. The main subject for discussion was most

difficult and most controversial. It had been the subject of a
protracted battle between him and the Chiefs of Staff, and
although on this night he finally accepted their view he did not
do so without a final battery of scorn and abuse. Most of this
was directed at the C.I.G.S., not only, I felt, because he was the
Chairman of the Chiefs of Staffs Committee, but because he
was the most irascible of the three, the most likely to be
provoked into counter-attack. So it turned out and there was a
vigorous set-to—the C.I.G.S. letting off bullets of indignation
at machine-gun rate. 'What is he saying? He goes so fast,'
muttered to General Ismay, served only to increase the flow and
led to direct intervention: 'What is the matter, C.I.G.S.? If
you're going to get so cross I shall get cross too.' During these
exchanges there was very little point in taking notes and I sat
awkwardly and self-consciously, fearing that the Prime
Minister's rising anger might in some way fasten itself upon my
unknown but harmless head. The storm at last died away and a
tense uncomfortable silence ensued, broken at last by the Prime
Minister enquiring with unexpected brightness, 'You didn't
know that the Foreign Secretary and I were going to Moscow,
did you?' The Chiefs of Staff did not know it and they sat up in
surprise. Their surprise greatly delighted the Prime Minister,
who felt that after all he had scored off them. He went on to
add with boyish delight, 'And the C.I.G.S. did not know he was
coming with us.' As for the Chiefs, their anger and resentment
were turned at once into practical solicitude about his safety, his
flying route, type of aeroplane, etc.; and the meeting ended in
most friendly good humour to such a degree that the C.I.G.S.,
forgetting the storm, noted in his diary: 'We were lucky to find
the Prime Minister in a very reasonable and quiet mood.'

Apart from this occasion my contacts with him during the
war were not direct. I would occasionally meet him in the
passages of those underground offices where a good many of us
worked and slept. He would give one a growling or smiling

c

'Good evening', according to his mood, or pass one by in fixed
and brooding taciturnity. Sometimes one would meet him on
the stairs carried aloft in his special chair by a couple of strong
marines. At the war-time conferences—at Cairo, at Quebec, at
Potsdam—he was more often visible to us than he was at home.
On our way to Cairo I travelled in *Renown* with him and well
do I remember his critical interest in some sessions of P.T.
which Captain Antony Buzzard organised for us on the
quarter-deck. The Prime Minister sat aloft and surveyed us
with amusement not unmixed with scorn; for most of us were
not very fit or agile after months of underground incarceration
in our offices. The sessions came to an abrupt end when the
progress of one of those rough-and-tumble games brought
about a situation in which a small and delicate W.R.N.S. officer
was supposed to carry an overweight soldier pick-a-back.

On our way to the second Quebec Conference in September
1944 the whole lot of us from the Prime Minister downwards—
other Ministers, Chiefs of Staff, General Ismay, Joint Planners,
other staff officers—travelled together in the *Queen Mary* from
the Clyde to Halifax, Nova Scotia. I had no close personal
contact with him during this voyage but his presence weighed
heavily upon us all. He was not in the best of health or the best
of moods. The weather was hot and muggy. Our course,
selected to be as submarine-free as possible, took us far to the
south and the Prime Minister complained bitterly of the sticky
heat. The sea had no business to be so torrid. The American
Admiral, 'Savvy' Cook, commenting upon this mood of dis-
pleasure and disapproval of the sea, said, 'I seem to have heard
of an English King in the past who tried unsuccessfully to
interfere with the sea.' The Prime Minister, as usual before these
mighty Conferences, was at variance with the Chiefs of Staff
and we, the Planners, were kept busy writing reports on this
and that and draft minutes of explanation which the Chiefs
might send forward to the Prime Minister—a lot of late-night

work, many voices raised in argument and the usual hurry and strain to get things done in time. On the return journey from New York the Chiefs of Staff were not all with us and the Prime Minister announced his intention of spending much time with the Planners. This was a situation he always hoped to bring about. The Planners were his, he obstinately averred, and he continued throughout the war to resent the assumption by the Chiefs of Staff—a perfectly correct assumption—that the Planners were responsible to them and to them alone. I foresaw some very uncomfortable discussions and some awkward clashes of loyalty during this return journey, but mercifully Providence ruled otherwise. The Prime Minister took the opportunity to rest for a day or two and the Planners were left in peace. It was just as well. It was much safer to be spared a sort of flirtation with the Prime Minister. He would have used all his arts of seduction to get us to espouse his causes and to find arguments to defeat the Chiefs of Staff. If we had refused his anger would have been very great and he would without doubt have demanded our instant dismissal. He did this from time to time in any case. By some mischance he would get hold of a Planners' report before it had been to the Chiefs of Staff and would demand to know the names of the officers responsible so that they might be summarily reprimanded. On one of our reports, which seemed to him to have a milk-and-water conclusion, he wrote: 'Who are the uniformed psalm-singing defeatists who wrote this report?' He did not love the Planners. They always found arguments against his most cherished schemes. Once years later Lord Cherwell gave me a prize for valour when he overheard me telling the Prime Minister that for the last two or three years of the war I had been Secretary of the Joint Planning Staff. He certainly gave me a baleful look, but that was all.

My closest glimpses of the Prime Minister at Potsdam I have recorded later in what I have written about Earl Attlee. After

he left Potsdam to take part in the General Election, I did not
see him again until he took office once more in October 1951.
I was then an Under-Secretary in the Cabinet Office working
directly under Sir Norman Brook. Mr. Churchill's return
caused a considerable alteration in planned appointments. Sir
Edward Bridges was about to retire and Sir Norman Brook
was to leave the Cabinet Office. Mr. Padmore (now Sir
Thomas) was to succeed Sir Norman Brook as Secretary of the
Cabinet. The Prime Minister would have none of this. Sir
Edward Bridges was an old and trusted friend. It was very inconsiderate of him to think of retiring at this juncture. Moreover, he could not contemplate having anyone as Secretary of
the Cabinet except Sir Norman Brook, a well-known and
experienced official. He had nothing whatever against Mr.
Padmore, and he had no doubt that he was an excellent official,
but he had never met him and it was not right or wise to expect
the Prime Minister on taking up office in such grave times to
waste his nervous energy in getting acquainted with somebody
new. Accordingly everyone stayed where he was. We had
similar difficulties over the principal private secretary at No. 10.
David Pitblado had recently been appointed to this position and
was, I imagine, somewhat excited and elated by the prospect
of serving Churchill at such close quarters. But the Prime
Minister, as usual, pined for old faces. Could he not have Sir
Leslie Rowan? No, he was far too senior now and could not be
spared from a position of paramount importance as head of the
Overseas Finance Division of the Treasury. The pouting mouth
showed that the Prime Minister thought nothing of greater
importance than serving him, but he let it pass and turned his
pursuit in the direction of Jock Colville, who had served as one
of his private secretaries for a part of the war. Jock Colville was
in fact rather too junior in rank for this position and he was,
moreover, serving as First Secretary in the British Embassy at
Lisbon and looking forward at that time to a career in the

Foreign Service. It was felt, however, that the Prime Minister was likely to regard these obstacles as trivial and insignificant. Accordingly Jock Colville was extracted from Lisbon and brought back to London. Bridges then went to the Prime Minister and told him that Colville was now available and that he would transfer Pitblado elsewhere. 'You don't think Mr. Pitblado will have any regrets, do you?' the Prime Minister enquired with tender solicitude. 'Well, naturally he will,' said Bridges. 'It doesn't fall to everyone's lot to serve you in such an intimate capacity and of course he had been looking forward to it.' Mr. Churchill's compassion immediately prevailed. 'Pray let him stay, then,' he said, 'and we will have two joint principal private secretaries.' And so it was and only men of good sense and good taste could have made it work.

At the time of Mr. Churchill's return to office Lieutenant-General Sir Kenneth Maclean was Chief Staff Officer to the Minister of Defence and as Mr. Churchill once again assumed the role of Minister of Defence he was necessarily in close contact with General Maclean. He had nothing against General Maclean, a good-looking, balanced, intelligent and experienced officer, but he wanted old faces as usual. He could not have Pug Ismay because he had already made him Secretary of State for Commonwealth Relations. Very well, then could he not have Ian Jacob? He was advised, earnestly and persuasively, to give General Maclean a chance. He was a very distinguished officer and if he was summarily removed his career was bound to suffer. Besides, Ian Jacob had left the Army and was now Director of Overseas Broadcasting in the B.B.C. There would be a good many technical difficulties about bringing him back into the Army, especially at one rank above his retired rank of Major-General. The Prime Minister found none of these arguments convincing and he fought a persistent and vigorous battle to get Ian Jacob back. He did not altogether take to General Maclean, chiefly because he had never had anything to

do with him in the past and because he had made up his mind
to have Jacob. He liked Jacob and he was used to him. He liked
his strong and lucid intellect, his grasp of detail, his air of unruffled and unhasting efficiency. He admired, perhaps, Ian
Jacob's character, so utterly different from his own, the stoic
calm, the absolute self-control, the mistrust of exaggerated and
excessive emotion, nothing too much of anything. Of course,
the Prime Minister won. Everything was arranged. Only the
date for the change had to be fixed. Should it be before or
after the visit which the Prime Minister was about to make to
the U.S.A. and Canada? We were due to sail at the end of
December and a few days before the Prime Minister had still
not made up his mind. Should he be accompanied by General
Maclean or General Jacob? The moment arrived when a
decision had to be made. Passports, inoculations, clothes,
families, press releases and all that—mercifully they forced a
decision in the end. Brook and I had Maclean waiting in the
United Services Club at 10 p.m. and Ian Jacob in the Army and
Navy Club at the same time, waiting to receive the decision.
Once again the Prime Minister's compassion prevailed. It would
be too unkind and inconsiderate to deprive General Maclean of
the trip. General Jacob could take over on our return.

And so we set off. Once again we all travelled in the *Queen
Mary* but not without a good deal of initial doubt and trouble.
As we were about to sail, the *Queen Mary* fouled her anchor and
we were delayed all of twenty-four hours. This was most un-
popular. The Prime Minister was impatient to get on and at
once demanded that aeroplanes should be provided and that
the whole delegation, with all its secret files and cabinets, now
so carefully and securely organised in cramped cabins, should
disembark and make its way to an airfield. Nobody liked this
idea, from Lord Moran, the Prime Minister's doctor, to the
baggage master and security officers. At length the Prime
Minister was persuaded to stay patiently where he was and

Gordon Selwyn, then Dean of Winchester, sent his cathedral choir over to beguile the time and soften the Prime Minister's anger with carol-singing. It was a very charming occasion, but I do not think the Prime Minister was present. When at last we did sail we encountered very heavy seas for the first two days, but by New Year's Eve the weather was fair and the Prime Minister gave an agreeable party to all of us in his state rooms.

This visit to the United States so soon after his election was entirely characteristic. His thoughts flew back to the war-time alliance and the war-time conferences. He felt that the Attlee Government had not fostered Anglo-American friendship, had even let it cool off, and he was most anxious if he could to establish the same close links with President Truman as he had had with Roosevelt. He wanted the Chiefs of Staff to do the same thing and the C.I.G.S., Field Marshal Slim, and the First Sea Lord, Admiral McGrigor, were in the delegation with us. The whole thing was given a further war-time flavour by the inclusion of Anthony Eden, invariably present at war-time conferences, Pug Ismay, now Secretary of State for Commonwealth Relations, and Lord Cherwell. Apart from these Ministers there were well-known faces amongst the officials too —Brook himself, Leslie Rowan, a war-time private secretary, and Roger Makins and Jock Colville called back from the Foreign Service to be private secretary again. It was like old times and surely the Americans would welcome these old faces and the warm links would be renewed. It was not to be. The Americans were hospitable, as they always are, and friendly, and some useful and successful negotiations took place, but there were different names and different powers and different influences.

The trip left some vivid recollections in my mind and memory. We were all disembarked as we went up the Hudson River into tenders and put ashore at Brooklyn. It was very early in the morning and very cold. We were assembled in a large

Customs shed; there to be officially welcomed on to the sacred soil of the United States. A military band played the ceremonial anthems very loud and the noise reverberated discordantly round the shed. But the ceremony was brief. The Prime Minister was impatient to get on, we had lost time already, and we were hurried on to waiting motor-cars. On the way reporters besieged those whom they could identify. One or two accosted me. 'Was I Lord Cherwell?' No, I was not, but I was pleased to point him out: large, erect, imperturbable, un-smiling, proceeding without haste or visible animation, arrayed in long black overcoat and black bowler hat—incon-gruous, inappropriate, strange, a figure of interest and surprise to Yankee newspapermen, who soon learnt, none the less, that the Professor was not to be coaxed into any form of communi-cation at all.

During this visit I entered the White House for the first time to attend the discussions between the Prime Minister and President Truman, more formal perhaps than Winston wanted. Truman was courteous and business-like, refusing to be drawn into detailed argument, avoiding any incautious step, conscious, it seemed to me, of the watchful eyes of his hard-faced advisers, afraid of being beguiled by Winston's rhetoric, the appeals to the comradeship of war, the joint sacrifices, the joint responsi-bilities, the ties of blood and history and the like, or by his display of charm, the wit, the smiles, the tears. It was clear to us that there was to be no renewal of the love affair. The war was over. There were other nations now besides the British, nations with equal claims on Uncle Sam's pocket, whose voices were deserving of equal attention. If we would take our place in the queue they would see what they could do for us. In fact after some fairly hard bargaining and tough negotiation we received great benefits from this visit and there was no doubt whatever of the continuing warmth of affection felt by the American people for Mr. Churchill. They were delighted that he was

once again our Prime Minister and I think it would be true
to say that our relationship with the Americans did begin to
gather warmth from the time of this visit. With the advent of
General Eisenhower to the White House it grew warmer still
and the first messages exchanged between him and Mr.
Churchill had all the war-time glow of comrades in arms.

Our method of progression from the British Embassy to the
White House for these meetings never failed to excite and
amuse Pug Ismay and me. A huge cavalcade of cars, with the
Prime Minister and Sir Oliver Franks, British Ambassador at the
time, in the leading one, would set off preceded, flanked and
followed up by countless outriders on noisy motor-cycles, all
with sirens and whistles. Off we would set with sirens blowing
hard all down Massachusetts Avenue, traffic scattering rapidly
or halting nervously at the side. Obeying no rules the cortège
swept from one side of the road to the other, swirled the wrong
way round squares and circles, intimidating and routing every
vehicle and every human being in our path, finishing in a
triumphant confusion of noise and bustle at the gates of the
White House.

From Washington we all flew up to Ottawa for discussions
with Mr. St. Laurent and the Canadian Government. Ottawa
was in deep snow and the cold was intense. We were made very
much at home. The occasion which remains clearest in my
mind is a luncheon given by the Governor-General, Earl
Alexander of Tunis, at Rideau Hall. There were perhaps forty
or fifty people in all and amongst them General Sir Gerald
Templer, as he then was, who had been sent for to meet the
Prime Minister in Ottawa. The Prime Minister wanted him to
go to Malaya with full civil and military powers, combining
in his own person the offices of High Commissioner and
Commander-in-Chief, and clear up the terrorist war. As he and
I stood chatting together before lunch he told me he had agreed
to go and it was clear to me that in his tense imaginative way he

was already grappling with countless problems in his mind. His
nerves were taut and his remarks more staccato than usual. An
A.D.C. approached with cocktails, collecting, as he walked
over the carpet in this intense cold, a great deal of electricity. As
General Templer took his cocktail, happening to touch the
A.D.C.'s hand, he received, in his tense state, a severe electric
shock which made him jump and shout. We went into lunch
and when it was over the Governor-General rose to his feet and
said that it was the Prime Minister's wish that he should on this
occasion officially announce General Templer's appointment.
After a few graceful compliments he invited us to drink the
General's health and wish him success. General Templer was
then called upon to reply. He was still tense and highly strung
and in nervous jerks he spat out at us: 'Thank you. I am going
to do a job and I won't say anything about it until I've done it.'
Upon which the Prime Minister beamed round the table,
calling out: 'There you are, you see. The General is a man of
deeds and not of words.'

My recollections of the Prime Minister over the next two
years are mainly of his performances at Cabinet meetings
which I attended regularly as Brook's assistant. I have a particular recollection of him also at a Commonwealth Prime
Ministers' meeting, but these meetings are a subject to which I
have devoted a separate chapter. In Cabinet he retained his skill.
He could be patient, conciliatory, cunning, short-tempered,
morose, procrastinating, contradictory, as the occasion demanded. He was always pugnacious and never very business-
like. As the Cabinet assembled he would announce that he
proposed to take the items in a different order. 'This is a subject
of such grave moment,' he would announce 'that I think the
Cabinet would wish to devote as much time as possible to it.
We will therefore take it first instead of fourth.' Then turning
to Brook he would say: 'You have, of course, invited the
Minister of Works? It is essential that he should be with us.' 'I

had invited the Minister of Works,' Brook would patiently explain, 'at twelve noon when I judged we should have reached this item, but now you have changed the order.' Ignoring this sane reasoning, the Prime Minister would continue to complain: 'But it must be obvious, Sir Norman, that we cannot embark upon these matters without the Minister responsible for the execution of our policy . . .' and so on; but by this time I was out of the door putting through fevered telephone calls to the Minister to get to No. 10 as fast as he could. This summoning of non-Cabinet Ministers to be in attendance for a particular item always led us into difficulties and trouble. It was impossible to judge the length of time any item would last. The most unexpected points of controversy would arise and what looked like a straightforward issue would be endlessly protracted. Alternatively what we thought a difficult and obstinate problem would be immediately resolved. The only safe rule was to ask these Ministers too early rather than too late, but it resulted, only too often, in some Ministers wasting a whole morning in the outer lobby and perhaps never being invited in at all. I still remember with shame that I invited Alec Home to attend for one item at a Cabinet meeting in August, as the Secretary of State for Scotland was away. He had to interrupt his grouse-shooting and come down from Scotland just for this purpose and it was not till we were nearly halfway through the item that I remembered about him and dashed out and fetched him in. He was not very pleased—and no wonder. But he forgave me and I had much to do with him in later years.

The Prime Minister took no greater account of time at these meetings than he did of the order of items on the Agenda. Unless he was officially engaged, his lunch would be served when he wanted it. He was not in the least disturbed by the increasing restiveness of certain Ministers, who doubtless had important luncheon engagements, as the clock moved on to 1.30 or later. Once I remember a private secretary interrupting the meeting (a very rare occurrence) to tell the Prime Minister that the Mahdi had arrived. 'Well, he must wait,' said the Prime Minister, and added: 'unless you think he will go off and make another revolt.'

He usually followed the general rule of proceedings. He would call on the responsible Minister to introduce his memorandum and would then invite the opinions of other Ministers most closely concerned, adding his own if the subject interested him. Where he was himself deeply moved and concerned he would fight hard to make his own view prevail. If he was clearly going to lose he would take refuge in procrastination, complaining to Brook that it was not wise to expect the Cabinet to reach a decision of such massive significance after a single discussion and that the matter should be put down again for the next meeting. Brook and I often suffered from this sort of thing, since we very well knew that the Departments concerned could not, for various reasons, wait another day for a decision. If Brook made a remonstrance to this effect the Prime Minister would then order a Cabinet for 10 p.m. that day, much to everyone's annoyance. But he did not mind. It would give him time to do some personal canvassing and there was a greater chance of his colleagues acquiescing if they were particularly anxious not to meet for a long time late at night.

Once, I remember, when he had his back to the wall in Cabinet he employed a different technique. It was the day that Lord Woolton, after a severe illness and long absence, returned to the Cabinet. The Prime Minister could find no support for his point of view. He pouted resentfully and began to ask each Minister in turn, but it was always the same reply: 'No, Prime Minister, I am afraid I cannot agree.' The atmosphere became very tense. The less confident Ministers shuffled and looked down uneasily, but they stuck to their guns. The turn came to Lord Woolton. 'And now, Lord President, what is your view?' said the Prime Minister, and went on at once: 'And perhaps I may say how rejoiced we are to have you with us again, how much we have missed your wise counsel, and how greatly we have admired the courage and fortitude with which you have faced your grievous afflictions—and I am not putting all this in just to get you on my side!' The tension snapped and whether the Prime Minister got his way or not his colleagues forgot their antagonism and thought what a wonderful and lovable old man he was.

He was not merciful. If he thought any of his colleagues lacking in political courage he would not hesitate to point it out. 'Never apologise to the other side,' he would say. 'It is quite unnecessary to debase yourself.' Or 'You are afraid to eat your words. There is no need to be. I have eaten a great many of mine in my time and on the whole I have found them a most wholesome diet.'

When Brook was absent for one reason or another I had the rather daunting privilege of sitting next to the Prime Minister at Cabinet and other meetings. Generally the meetings went smoothly and in accordance with a well-worn routine and careful preparation. Sometimes it was necessary to point out that an item on the Agenda had been missed or to push before the Prime Minister a copy of the brief which he had somehow mislaid. Such minor and trivial interferences had to be tactfully and delicately managed. It was not difficult to bring down on yourself an angry retort: 'What is it you are doing? I am well aware of the business. You should hold your tongue and attend to your menial task.' Interventions by officials or officers, even when they were members of a committee, were not greatly encouraged or very patiently heard. Admiral Evans-Lombe once displayed extraordinary courage at some committee meeting. After giving a short professional discourse on the naval aspects of a particular problem he continued: '. . . From the political point of view——' and was violently interrupted by the Prime Minister: 'The political point of view is nothing

to do with you, Admiral. You would be better employed trying to improve your professional skill. You can leave political
matters to us. It would be a much safer world if Admirals and
Generals stuck to their last.' 'Yes, Prime Minister,' said Evans-
Lombe. 'As I was saying, from the political point of view . . .'
And somehow he got away with it. This was courage indeed in
the face of a very angry enemy.

I myself displayed very little courage in the face of the
Prime Minister—the only man, I think, in my adult life of
whom I have been afraid. But once during a Commonwealth
Prime Ministers' Conference there was a very small meeting
summoned to discuss a controversial subject. It was summoned
for 6 p.m. and the only persons present were the Prime Minister
in the Chair, Lord Salisbury, Mr. Butler and Earl Alexander,
together with Mr. Menzies, the Prime Minister of Australia,
and Mr. Holland, the Prime Minister of New Zealand. Brook
was unable to go and I acted as Secretary. On the whole the
discussion was less prickly and the atmosphere less stormy than
I had expected and as the clock reached 7.00 I began to feel that
we had come securely to a reasonable understanding. Perhaps
it was this rather unexpected result which made the Prime
Minister say: 'Well, I think before we adjourn we should agree
a communiqué. Lord Salisbury, you are very adept in these
matters. What do you think might be included?' If I had fore-
seen this I would have had a draft with me, but I had nothing.
Lord Salisbury, who was surprised to find himself described as
adept in such matters, gave forth a few ideas, and Mr. Menzies,
Mr. Holland, Mr. Butler and the Prime Minister added a few
more. Anybody who has listened to this sort of thing will
know how confusing it soon becomes. Turning to me, the
Prime Minister said, 'Now you will go next door and dictate
a draft as speedily as possible and bring it back for our consideration.' Before I could rise from my chair, Mr. Menzies was
saying: 'I am sorry. It is getting late. I have a dinner engage-

ment and I fear I cannot wait.' The Prime Minister looked a little put out and acting on a momentary impulse of rash courage I said, 'I think I have the ideas in my mind and I think I could read out a draft to you now.' The Prime Minister was doubtless surprised at my arrogance and by way of encouragement enjoined me in intimidating tones, 'Very well, then, but mind you get it right.' I did get it right, or right enough to satisfy Mr. Menzies, who fled from the room. I went back to the Cabinet Office to write the minutes and issue the communiqué. Instantly my phone rang. The Prime Minister wished to see the communiqué before it was issued—but all was well.

A shattering morning came. Brook was ill and there was a Cabinet meeting. I went across, as usual, to No. 10 and waited with the Cabinet Ministers in the lobby outside the Cabinet room. Presently we were summoned in, not as usual by the Prime Minister himself, but by one of the private secretaries, and we took our seats. I was anxious, as usual in Brook's absence, anxious that everything should go smoothly, that the right Ministers should arrive at the right time, that I should be alert to the points made in discussion, able to dictate a draft—if any such were needed—afraid that the Prime Minister would find me a fumbling and ineffective substitute for Brook. There was an uncomfortable feeling in the room, a lifeless, heavy air, and the Prime Minister was still, silent and brooding. It was clear at once, as soon as he attempted to start the first item, that he was exhausted or ill. He could hardly shape his words to introduce the subject, he gave no lead and reached no conclusion. He fumbled ineffectually with his papers. His sense of touch had gone. He struggled on, scarcely comprehending what he was called upon to do. His colleagues sat in dismay, reluctant to speak at all, thinking it not worth while to express a point of view, wondering only in silent consternation what was the matter with the old man. Somehow he finished what was necessary and with great relief we made out from his mumbled incoherent speech that we should meet again next day to clear up the rest.

I went back to the Cabinet Office down-hearted and alarmed. I wrote the minutes, I made arrangements for the Cabinet meeting the next day and in the evening went down to recount the melancholy tale to Brook in his bed. At about 11 p.m. that night the private secretaries at No. 10 rang me up in my flat, enquiring if it was really essential to have a Cabinet meeting the next day. The Prime Minister was very tired. They wanted to get him out of London as soon as they possibly could. Would it be possible to postpone the meeting? 'Of course,' I said, beginning to suspect the real truth of the matter, 'it is quite possible and I will cancel it forthwith.' They could not say more over the telephone. They would tell me more later.

He had had a stroke the night before, not the first but the worst. He had insisted, nevertheless, on getting up and going through with the Cabinet meeting. It had been too much for him and at last he had surrendered to the importuning of his family, Charles Moran, his doctor, and his personal staff, and had consented to go down to Chartwell. His recovery was remarkable. In a month he was back in London, presiding over a Cabinet meeting held in the state dining-room at No. 10. The Cabinet room was being decorated. He was lively and cheerful. There was a very slight thickness of speech which soon disappeared and his gait was a little uncertain; he faltered now and then as he stumped vigorously along.

Indomitable heart, indomitable head, indomitable body, in imagination inspired, in execution most powerful, in humour most rich, his genius most varied and versatile, in experience matchless—of all Englishmen the greatest.

Earl Attlee

I was certainly not alone in believing in the years before the war that chance had brought Mr. Attlee into the leadership of the Labour Party and that as soon as the party had recovered from the disaster of 1931 he would be painlessly dispossessed and left in the ranks of mediocrity to which in the eyes of most men he seemed to belong. In those days it certainly never occurred to me—or I should think to anyone else—that he ever could in any combination of circumstances become Prime Minister of this country. I had never seen him and knew nothing of him at first hand, but his rather uninspiring speeches were enough to confirm the prevalent opinion that he had no political future of any importance. It is a matter of history that this was a complete misjudgment, but even now nobody can really understand or explain how it was done, how this apparently humdrum figure not only retained the leadership of his highly volcanic party but as Prime Minister carried out a social revolution in this country and a constitutional revolution in the Empire. Nobody can really explain it—least of all Earl Attlee himself, who seems to see it all as the result more of chance than design. At least when he gave us his autobiography, modestly, searching for a title, he chose one by which he seemed to disclaim any ambitions or intentions of his own—'As it happened'. Part of his strength is, of course, this very modesty, together with that dry humour which prompted him to describe this book in private conversation as 'a pedestrian little work'.

I saw a little of Mr. Attlee during the war. He was occasionally to be seen in the War Cabinet Offices visiting the Map Room, going to meetings, etc., and sometimes we were told to examine and report on some strategic idea which he had submitted to the

Prime Minister and which the Prime Minister thought it polite, and politic, to have examined. For myself I often found his opinions rather sensible and admirably expressed with terse brevity, but it was the fashion amongst us to regard him as a lightweight and to dismiss his observations as either obvious or silly. My increasingly good opinion of him was confirmed when I found myself attending, as one of the Secretariat, a Cabinet committee over which the Prime Minister had appointed him to preside. The subject was, I think, shipping in some form or other and the members of the committee included A. V. Alexander, the First Lord, Lord Leathers, the Minister of Transport, various other Ministers and some high-ranking officers from the three Services. The subject was technical and difficult and there were probably very few people in the room who had the facts and issues clearly in their heads, but there was no doubt whatever who was in the chair. Any long-winded irrelevance was summarily checked and Ministers who became garrulous with their neighbours—it was after dinner—were sharply called to order. This was the last sort of chairmanship I had expected to see and my admiration was greatly increased. I was to see a lot more of it during Mr. Attlee's Premiership.

For all that, anyone working amongst us who had prophesied in 1944 or early 1945 that Mr. Attlee would beat Mr. Churchill in a General Election in 1945 would have been thought eccentric to the point of lunacy. Mr. Churchill overshadowed all. He had his finger in every pie. He led and he ruled and he seemed—and of course, so long as the war lasted, was—indispensable. But we, who worked in this very small central core and knew all the secrets and thought ourselves mighty fine fellows, were entirely out of touch with public opinion. We had very little idea what the ordinary man in the street thought about 'after the war' and none at all about what the private soldier thought. My eyes were not opened until we went to the

Potsdam Conference in July 1945 and Mr. Churchill took Mr. Attlee with him just in case the election produced an unexpected result.

There was a victory parade by British troops on the Charlotten Strasse. It was a remarkable occasion—a march past of triumphant British troops and tanks along this German processional route; and all around devastation, scorched grass, burnt trees, houses in rubble and woebegone scavenging figures searching for anything in the wreck and ruin which might make their lives less insupportable. On specially erected stands were assembled the great figures of the war—the Prime Minister himself, Mr. Attlee, Mr. Eden, the Chiefs of Staff, Field Marshal Montgomery and other great Commanders-in-Chief, prominent commanders and staff officers, a glittering company to watch this symbol of British triumph. Along the route were soldiers of the 2nd Army, British soldiers not on duty and many inquisitive German civilians pressing against the cordon of military police who lined the route. I had expected to feel the familiar surge of patriotic emotion with extreme intensity. There was every cause and every occasion to feel it, but too much had happened, too much was lost, and I think that we all 'affected more emotion than we felt'. When the parade was over two very curious things happened. The V.I.P.s descended from their stand and as they walked across the processional way they were greeted with acclamation and applause by the great audience of British soldiers. It was clear to me at once that Mr. Attlee, in spite of his graceless, awkward bearing, shuffling along on his small, outward-pointing feet, grinning and smiling like a ventriloquist's doll, was more warmly cheered than Mr. Churchill, and for the first time I saw the writing on the wall.

If the British crowd seemed to exhibit a strange preference for Mr. Attlee there was no doubt about the feelings of the Germans. Almost immediately they broke through the cordon and surrounded Mr. Churchill with shouts and cheers. This must have been an anxious moment for the security police. Any revengeful German could easily have killed Mr. Churchill on the spot, but to our great relief their mood was cheerful and friendly and they seemed anxious to applaud the man who, more than any other, had brought them to misery and humiliation.

A few days later Mr. Churchill, Mr. Attlee, Mr. Eden and nearly the whole of the United Kingdom delegation went home to vote. I was left behind with a few others to mind the shop and to make it ready for the new Prime Minister and Foreign Secretary whoever they might be. I had begun to have secret doubts about the issue but these were not shared by anyone else—least of all by Stalin, who scoffed openly when Mr. Churchill assured him that the result was not a foregone conclusion. During the days of waiting for the result I spent a good deal of time with friends in the American delegation who were absolutely convinced that Mr. Churchill had nothing to fear. When the results came through the Americans were staggered and angry. They had always thought the British, for all their failings, were sporting people. How could they show such gross ingratitude? How could they repudiate the man to whom they owed their survival as a nation? It was not only hopelessly foolish but criminal. I could offer no satisfactory explanation and I was acutely conscious during these days that my most intimate American friends found it hard to forgive me or to receive me with their customary warmth. I believe that when Englishmen woke and up found what they had done many of them felt some sense of guilt and shame. They wanted a change, they wanted to give Mr. Attlee a show, but they had never intended to cause misery and humiliation to the old man. But it was not a bad instinct, after all. The man who was primarily responsible for winning the war would find it hard to switch his great talents to winning the peace. The war had been a tremendous upheaval. A new kind of society was needed; let the other party—the reforming, idealistic party— have a go at it. That was how men thought. They did not regard it as Churchill versus Attlee. If that had been the true and only issue I do not think Mr. Attlee, comparatively unknown and without popular gifts, would have had a chance.

I did not stay in Potsdam after the return of Mr. Attlee with Mr. Bevin. The military part of that conference was already concluded and I was sent back to help to finish the job in London and in Washington. In November 1945 I was de-mobilised and spent about seven months right away from the centre of government, quite unburdened by secrets and quite unaware of the performance of the new Ministers. When I returned to government service in mid-1946 it was to a position where I saw little of Mr. Attlee in person. My closer impressions of him belong in the main to 1950 and 1951.

One authentic story of his early days in No. 10 is worth recording. It was the custom at first to refer to him as 'the little man'. There was perhaps an element of the patronising about this but it never implied any lack of respect. At this time he had a private secretary named J. T. A. Burke—before the war with the Victoria and Albert Museum and now Professor of Fine Arts at the University of Melbourne—and the patronage secretary was, and remained for many years to come, Tony Bevir—later Sir Antony Bevir. Burke had a very small son for whom he betrayed much paternal solicitude and, like all fathers, supposed that his friends were almost equally solicitous and interested. Upon return from leave in Ireland on one occasion Tony Bevir enquired of Burke, 'And how is the little man?' To which Burke replied, 'He is all right now but we have had a lot of trouble with him.' 'Trouble?' said Tony Bevir. 'What sort of trouble?' 'Well,' Burke explained, 'he gets strange notions into his head and nothing will persuade him that they are false.' 'Dear me!' said Tony, 'this sounds very serious. I knew there might be some anxieties at first but I hoped that time and experience would teach him stability and caution. But can you give me an example of these strange notions?' 'Well, the other day,' said Burke, 'he said that he had swallowed nails and drawing-pins.' 'Swallowed nails and drawing-pins! Whatever did you do?' 'We rushed him off to hospital and they X-rayed him but there was nothing to be seen. So they gave him a good dose and he seems to be all right again.' Tony Bevir's amazement was extreme—'You've told Bridges, of course, haven't you?' 'Told Bridges? Why ever should I?' said the astonished father—and at that point, but not before, the cross-purposes became plain.

I had one slight contact with Mr. Attlee in the days when I was Secretary General of the Brussels Treaty Defence Organisation. The United Kingdom Minister of Defence, Mr. A. V. Alexander, gave a cocktail party at Admiralty House for all the delegations. It was a helpful gesture in those early days and it was still more helpful when he persuaded the Prime Minister to be present. At Mr. Alexander's request I acted as a sort of catalyst on this occasion, hopping about and trying to make men of different nationalities overcome their shyness and talk to each other in one language or another. At the start I stood by the Prime Minister, who told me with a wry look that his French was rusty and imperfect. I wanted him to talk to General Ely, but General Ely's shyness and modesty in the presence of the British Prime Minister made him reticent even in his own tongue and the Prime Minister never got beyond a brisk handshake and a muttered '*Enchanté*'. Attlee's presence there and his smiling, if somewhat dumb, approach to people gave this infant organisation stimulus and encouragement and helped to convince the hesitant and doubting continental members that Britain really meant business.

From June 1950, when I returned to the Cabinet Office, to the fall of the Labour Government in the autumn of 1951, I had opportunities of watching Mr. Attlee from an official level. My contacts were never important. I was in no sense an intimate and trusted adviser, but sometimes in the absence of Sir Norman Brook or of Air Chief Marshal Sir William Elliot I sat by the Prime Minister at meetings, more particularly meetings on defence questions. During this period defence questions were crucial and controversial. It was the period of the Korean war. One of these defence meetings had a notorious consequence. We met late—after dinner—and continued late in great argument and perplexity. The Chiefs of Staff, basing themselves upon intelligence estimates of Chinese and Russian strengths and intentions, were asking for more—more money, more resources, more men. It is never easy for any Government to accept the military need and retard the provision of more and more welfare and prosperity, and Nye Bevan, then Minister of Labour, attempted to ridicule these intelligence estimates as grossly exaggerated and alarmist and no sound basis for such momentous policy decisions. The meeting ended in indecision. The argument of the Chiefs of Staff was at least not yet lost and Marshal of the Royal Air Force Sir John Slessor, then Chief of the Air Staff, saw a possible opportunity to press home his view against the doubts of Nye Bevan. Making his way with difficulty round the Cabinet room, contending, in spite of his game leg and stick, with the obstacles of pushed-back chairs and groups of still argumentative Ministers, he caught Nye Bevan at the door and asked him there and then to come and have a drink. As I saw them setting off together in good humour with each other I felt encouraged and hopeful. Whatever the outcome this was the right relationship between Ministers and Service chiefs. Jack Slessor, as he subsequently explained to me, calculated hastily that it was probably too late to get a drink at the Senior—there would be delays and interruptions and ringing

of bells. At White's all would be easy and he would be able
to sit quietly in some isolated corner with the Minister and give
emphatic utterance to his strong conviction. So it turned out.
All would have been well but for a couple of members, with
less liberal views and less serious purposes than Jack Slessor,
who insulted Nye Bevan as he left the club. It cannot reasonably
be alleged that this display of bad manners led to Bevan's
subsequent resignation and many years of tears and tribulations
for the Labour Party. That would be an absurd overestimate of
the importance of the incident. Yet many woes can be attributed
to the bad manners of the English upper classes. I have heard it
said that Cecil Beaton once asked Wavell (it seems a strange
conjunction of personalities) to what single factor he chiefly
attributed the loss of the Indian Empire. 'To the bad manners
of the British,' said Wavell in his dry laconic way—and it is
worth pondering.

Mr. Attlee liked defence questions and in some ways was at
his best in dealing with them. He had been a fighting soldier in
the first world war and he retained a marked affection for the
Army and some professional pride in its achievements. He was
sharp and impatient when his Ministerial colleagues made
contemptuous references to the Services. In consequence he was
popular with his Service chiefs and even Field Marshal
Montgomery is good enough to pat him on the back. They
liked his crisp manner, and all of them, I think without
exception, felt in sympathy and at ease with him.

This attachment which he felt to the Army and the vivid
associations with it stored up in his mind since the first war had
some interesting and curious consequences. Not only did he
defend the Army against the sneers of some of his colleagues
but he defended it in the vernacular. This rather mild-looking,
withdrawn Prime Minister became Major Attlee, the infantry
officer, letting off without restraint in the mess. 'What the hell
do you mean?' he would suddenly say. 'You can keep your

bloody sneers to yourself. Some of us are damned proud of the
British Army.' This sort of sally was not infrequent and caused
great surprise and some offence amongst Socialist Ministers.

Once, in Brook's absence, I was in attendance at a very small
meeting of Ministers at No. 10—the Prime Minister in the
chair, Ernie Bevin, Mr. Shinwell, then Minister of Defence,
and perhaps one or two others. The discussion was about the
French, their political instability, the deficiencies of their armed
forces, etc. Someone was suggesting that the French were very
critical of us, that they expected us to do far more for the
defence of Western Europe than we were doing, and so on.
'What the hell right have they got to criticise us?' he shouted:
'Tell them to go and clear up their own bloody stable. They
haven't any decent generals. They haven't had a good general
since Prince Eugene and he served their enemies.' Mr. Shinwell
ventured to put in, 'Some people think General de Lattre is
pretty good,' and Uncle Ernie added: 'You'd better ask old
Mallaby here. He knows all about de Lattre.' Bristling slightly
the Prime Minister turned expectantly to me. Hastily selecting
some sort of definition I started, 'He is certainly unusual, lively,
colourful, dynamic.' 'Dynamic is he?' barked the Prime
Minister. 'I know what you mean. Just like General Nivelle—
gets us all killed.'

I would not myself subscribe to the widely held view that
Mr. Attlee's great strength was his power of chairmanship,
that he presided ably and constructively over his Cabinet. I do
not think that this was so. Certainly he was in charge. There
was no doubt about that and any Minister who was unable to
give sensible answers to questions about his own Department
was soon in trouble—'It is no good your coming here so ill-
prepared and wasting everyone's time.' I never heard Churchill
speak to his colleagues in this magisterial fashion—to officials,
yes, but not to Ministerial colleagues. Mr. Attlee was fairly free
with rebuffs of this kind and in consequence the proceedings at

Cabinet and at Cabinet Committee meetings were usually orderly and brisk. Attention was paid to the Agenda and to the order in which the items were to be discussed. The time-table was adhered to. The meetings ended on time. The business was concluded. But there was nothing very constructive about all this. The Prime Minister was attentive to his brief. He introduced the subject in sensible, unimaginative terms and asked the right Ministers in the right order to express their views. He listened, or appeared to listen, patiently and fairly attentively, though he doodled incessantly. When the discussion was finished his summing-up was often blurred and incomplete and he rarely produced any constructive ideas of his own or seemed to give a powerful lead. His chairmanship was only a negative success. He was like a schoolmaster who kept order very well but did not really teach you very much. I do not think that the secret of his success lay here.

He had, at any rate in the early days of his administration, a strong team—Stafford Cripps, with far more powerful intellectual equipment, Ernie Bevin, with a more expansive nature and more popular appeal, Herbert Morrison, with a much stronger administrative sense, and Nye Bevan, with eloquence of a totally different and more splendid order. He knew this; he knew his own limitations, but he knew theirs too. Not one of them could really have taken his place. Each one had too many enemies. Mr. Attlee had none. Moreover, if he lacked some of their particular strength, he lacked their weakness also. He was not coldly intellectual, a sea-green incorruptible, he was not ruthless or sly and cunning, he was not emotional and unstable. So long as he remained himself—intelligent, industrious, modest, orderly, courageous and transparently honest—he could rule them. He must on no account attempt to meet them on their own ground. He must never be on such close terms with them that his own points of inferiority became evident. He must hold himself aloof, keep them at arm's length, have no favourites and no special friends. This was the attitude he rigidly adopted. This was his strength. He managed very well without their friendship and their intimate counsel, and I should think that he successfully avoided feeling any twinge of affection for any of them—except for Ernie Bevin. But if Ernie Bevin knew he had a pull with the Prime Minister he never took advantage of it. He was entirely loyal and with his large and heavy hand crushed the pitiful intrigue against the Prime Minister, an intrigue which the Prime Minister in his aloof fastness disregarded with easy disdain. He supported himself by the fullest possible use of the position and prestige of the Prime Minister and that is a very firm and very powerful support. Whatever the constitutional position of the Prime Minister, in practice he is infinitely more than a *primus inter pares*. The deference accorded to any British Prime Minister by his Cabinet colleagues is very striking indeed. In small matters other Ministers will treat him with punctilious respect. For example, they will not dream of entering the Cabinet room until the Prime Minister himself comes out and invites them in. In larger matters they will pay special attention to his views and his leadership, with a strong inclination to sink their own opinions and defer to his. They will accept his reproofs. They will hurry, like schoolboys, to do his bidding. Mr. Attlee knew all these cards and played them pretty well. He had, after all, seen at very close quarters the lavish exercise of these powers by the great Churchill himself. He had a good model to follow and on the whole he followed it well and in accordance with his natural gifts. But whereas Churchill struck hard and struck often, for ever returning to the attack, never letting an errant Minister get away with it, Mr. Attlee had much less follow-through. Like a wasp he buzzed in your face and stung you hard.

His dealings with officials, in so far as I was able to observe them, were for the most part equally impersonal. He could be sharp and irritable and he found it very hard indeed to make generous remarks or express gratitude. This does not mean that he did not feel it. In all ways he was more considerate than his predecessor but a great deal less stimulating. For myself I always had a strong feeling that there was no lack of affection in the man, that he would have liked to throw off the impenetrable armour of his office and to have a chat and a joke—there was plenty of humour—on easy terms. But he could not, or perhaps it was that he would not; for in occasional meetings with him in recent years he has been much more free with his opinions and much more ready with his caustic humour. I asked him not long ago what he thought of certain revelations then appearing in a Sunday paper. 'Frightful,' he said. 'I saw the author the other day and said, "I had no idea you were such a good writer of fiction." ' That is excellent and very characteristic, but not unnaturally in the days of his Premiership he kept these shots in his locker, or at any rate he did not repeat them to officials.

In recent years it has become the fashion to detect in him a kind of pungent wisdom, in his book reviews and in his occasional interventions in the House of Lords. People are inclined to say that he is not so colourless, after all. He never was, but after Churchill he seemed so, and in an age of broadcasting his rather poor attempts at oratory—that hot-potato voice, those staccato unarticulated phrases—were disastrous to the development of a popular personality. But he always had a definite personality, an individual shape and pattern—like one of his own doodles, an accurate, painstaking pattern, carefully drawn, carefully coloured, cleverly done, satisfying, attractive, comprehensive—never wild or confused or overpowering. I used to pinch these doodles at the end of meetings if I got the chance. One day he caught me at it. 'What are you doing?' he asked in a brusque tone of irritation. 'I was pinching your doodles, sir,' I said. 'I sell them for large sums of money.' His irritation gave place to something that was nearly a warm chuckle. He liked my cheek and he wished, I could not help feeling, that more people would talk to him like that, but he never knew how to make them.

Mr. Macmillan

Frequent and fruitful television appearances made Mr. Macmillan a very well-known figure. The drooping eye, the thick moustache, the bared teeth, the measured tones, the deviations back and forth from jollity to gravity, the genial bland Edwardian—he made a great popular appeal, which the nightly imitation at the Fortune Theatre did much to increase. The dull conventional English like a little individual eccentricity in their leaders—preferring Lloyd George's long-haired emotionalism to the gravitas of Asquith, Churchill's audacious gusto to the self-conscious rectitude of Neville Chamberlain, and Macmillan's vague self-deprecating avuncularity to the band-box style of Anthony Eden.

My own contacts with Mr. Macmillan were never very close or continuous, but what there were brought me a warm enjoyment. He is a man of cultivated taste and discernment, with a strong sense of history and tradition, relaxed, friendly and humorous in an Oxford-donnish sort of way. Nobody could ever suspect him of coming from Cambridge; and it is hard to suspect that he is himself any less blue-blooded than the family into which he married. His pride of ancestry is very great and the first time I ever spoke to him—in his room when he was Minister of Housing—he took up most of our official

time in showing me a picture of the lowly dwelling in the
Highlands from which his family sprang and explaining their
remarkable ascent to affluence.

On that day I found him engaging and attractive and I have
found him so ever since. I was the Secretary of a special
committee of Ministers and officials set up to help him to build
the 300,000 houses so rashly promised by his party in the 1953
election. It was my duty to brief him on the procedures at these
meetings and he was cunning enough to see that he might use
me and the Cabinet Office to help him get round some of the
difficulties he was encountering. He did it very well and very
charmingly. Officials like to be treated as human equals by
Ministers and he was particularly considerate and friendly, even
writing me a letter of sympathy when I was in hospital for a
small operation. He liked the oblique approach. He sent for you
because he wanted to see you, he liked your company, he
wanted to talk about his ancestry and yours, his Oxford days
and so on; and, as a sort of incidental offhand suggestion
muttered out not very clearly as he shuffled about the room,
perhaps you would be so good as to think up some way of
overcoming the obstruction being erected against him by some
Minister or Department.

Shortly before I went to New Zealand in 1957 to be High
Commissioner he sent for me to say goodbye. I went over to
No. 10 at the time appointed, protesting that I did not wish to
take up the Prime Minister's time. It was quite unnecessary for
him to see me if he was very busy. 'Busy!' said Freddie Bishop,
then his principal private secretary. 'He isn't busy. He is sitting
in there doing *The Times* crossword.' So he was, and this
imperturbable, or outwardly imperturbable, temperament is
one of his greatest assets. I went in and he took me off to his
small sitting-room upstairs, gave me a glass of sherry, assumed
that I had read Honour Moderations at Oxford, took down his
old Oxford texts and showed me his marginal annotations.

There we sat, rapt, back in the Oxford of the 1920's, caught up in the sense of kinship which a common education gives. From there he went on to talk of universities, their place in the national system of education, the extent of the Government's responsibility for them—matters with which he knew I had been closely concerned in the University Grants Committee. It was time to go before New Zealand was mentioned, but I managed to stammer out: 'You ought to come out. They always come here. No British Prime Minister in office has ever been there.' The vague stare and smile were intensified as he murmured, 'So glad; perhaps I'll see you.' And, of course, within a year he came.

He came, moreover, at a time of crisis in this country. Mr. Thorneycroft, then Chancellor of the Exchequer, had resigned on what he at any rate must have thought a matter of major consequence. With a wave of the hand Mr. Macmillan brushed this aside as a purely local difficulty, unimportant in comparison with the novel significance of a Commonwealth tour by a British Prime Minister in office. What an effective attitude this was! Poor Mr. Thorneycroft felt very small, or at least he seemed so. Chancellors do not resign every day and when they do Governments can be shaken and totter to their fall. But this time there was no crisis at all. Mr. Macmillan handed the job to Mr. Amory, got into his aeroplane and flew off to India. Mr. Thorneycroft crept out and not a dog barked. Meanwhile opinion in the Commonwealth was delighted to find a British Prime Minister attaching to Commonwealth affairs an importance far exceeding the importance of the financial and economic problems of the United Kingdom. It has always seemed to me that the unchallenged ascendancy which Mr. Macmillan at one time attained had its origin in this moment.

My wife and I had the agreeable task of accompanying Mr. Macmillan and Lady Dorothy throughout their eight-day tour of New Zealand. It was agreeable for many reasons. It was an

opportunity to revisit many places already known to us and
to renew former acquaintanceships. It was an opportunity to
judge at first hand the reactions of leading New Zealand Labour
politicians and of the ordinary New Zealander to the physical
presence of a British Prime Minister—and an old-fashioned
Conservative one at that. It was an opportunity to be in the
daily company of Mr. Macmillan's staff, some of whom were
old and dear friends of ours in London, and finally it was an
opportunity to get to know this remarkable man and his very
charming wife.

I was a little apprehensive at first. The start was unpromising.
On arrival in Auckland Mr. Macmillan was not very well; he
had a chill and a slight temperature, he was tired, tired of
making speeches, tired of dinners, tired of talking and tired of
flying. His failure to get out of his aeroplane during a short
fuelling stop in Australia had given rise to some ill-informed
and ill-deserved criticism in the Australian Press. I could not
help feeling that much the best thing would be to pack him
straight off to bed after dinner in the Grand Hotel and hope
that he would be fit for the rigours of the morrow. I felt it the
more strongly as dinner proceeded. Mr. Nash, the New
Zealand Prime Minister, sat next to him and for once it
seemed to me that that old man's tact and charm deserted him.
He did not seem to sense Mr. Macmillan's fatigue and quite
contrary to my hopes and expectations he missed the deep
significance of the occasion—the arrival for the first time in
history of a British Prime Minister in New Zealand. Some
quiet and elevated observations would have met the case, but
instead of this Mr. Nash became the party politician, trying to
provoke, with old outmoded sneers, the elegant leader of the
British Conservative Party. Mr. Macmillan was clearly put out
and had genuine difficulty, I thought, in concealing his irritation. When at last the uncomfortable meal ended I had a hasty
word with Norman Brook and Alister McIntosh, Mr. Nash's

chief adviser, and suggested that the serious political talk which was then to take place between the two Prime Ministers should be postponed. They thought we had better stick to the arrangement and they were right. For as the discussion proceeded and Brook and McIntosh and I grew more and more weary and less and less able to concentrate, the two Prime Ministers, after the manner of politicians, grew more and more animated as the clock approached midnight. Mr. Nash had quite laid aside his petty spiteful weapons and listened with thoughtful interest to Mr. Macmillan's account of his experiences in India. The atmosphere changed completely and wisdom, wit and friendliness, which both men possessed in good measure, soon prevailed. It was very late before they were willing to part.

Thereafter all went well. The New Zealand Government had planned the visit with imagination and good sense. Enough time must be allotted to political discussion but points of controversy were few and far between—the perennial anxiety about the price of butter, that long-distance combat between the British housewife and the New Zealand dairy-farmer, nuclear-bomb tests about which Mr. Nash, for all his latent pacifism, was sound and generous but had to face an actively hostile fringe, import restrictions hurtful to us but essential for the New Zealand economy, and a few others. These matters must be hammered out in Wellington and there also Mr. Macmillan must make a major political speech at a state luncheon. Then there must be speeches and receptions at the other three big cities—Auckland, Dunedin and Christchurch. All this was cut down to a minimum and the rest of the programme was devised with two main objects—to let the Macmillans see as much as possible of the true New Zealand, the farms, the rivers, the mountains, the thermal regions, the sea coasts, and to give them some rest and relaxation.

Accordingly our stay in Auckland was brief—too brief for the taste of the Aucklanders, who are in no doubt that their

E

city is the most important in New Zealand. After a mayoral reception we sped southwards in a cortège of cars through the rich farmlands of the Waikato, calling upon King Koroki of the Manipoto tribe at Turangawaewae on the way and receiving a traditional Maori welcome, lunching at Hamilton by the banks of that lovely Waikato River, with a brief unintended stop at Cambridge, imposed upon us by a resolute mayor who led his citizens at the double up the main street, bringing our cars to a sudden halt. From Cambridge, one of the most English of New Zealand places, with its hardwood trees and its village green, on to the land of geysers and hot lakes and subterranean rumblings to stay the night in the Wairakei Hotel. Here late after dinner we introduced Lady Dorothy to the hot swimming-pool where contrary to usual practice you must get out to cool down and get in to warm up again. Lady Dorothy loved it and returned for more before breakfast. The Prime Minister was too busy and not yet really fit, but he was fascinated next morning by the thunderous bore-holes which tap the natural sources of heat and power just below the earth's surface for the generation of electric power—a scheme spectacular and exciting. From this violent and potent combination of Man and nature we turned aside to see the natural beauty of the Huka Falls, then down on along the shores of Lake Taupo, paradise of fishermen, over the desert road by the foothills of Ruapehu and Ngauruhoe, grim desolate country, stopping for lunch at Waiouru, then along the windings of the Rangitikei Gorge, on to Bulls for tea and so to Wellington by the western coastal strip.

Mr. Macmillan enjoyed it all. The weather was fine and hot, the country richly diversified, mountains, lakes, rivers, green pasturelands, rank brown desert country and the Tasman Sea for once blue and peaceful; the people everywhere smiling and friendly, standing in the streets of their little townships, coming from their caravans and camping sites to wave a friendly welcome to the British Prime Minister. It was hard not to be moved and at each stop Mr. Macmillan made short smiling speeches and vague gestures of friendship to little knots of people—'I bring you affectionate greetings from the old country . . .' he would start—a genuine and sincere phrase which after constant iteration throughout New Zealand caused Lady Dorothy to beg him to try to find another. At Waiouru, where we lunched, he was delighted to be confronted with a strange New Zealand custom, the provision on the table of dry unmixed mustard. He chose cold ham and wanted mustard. What should he do? 'Mix it,' I said, and with my aid he did. He put some dry mustard in a large spoon, I dropped little drops of water on to it and he mixed and stirred vigorously with a fork. The process—which Lady Dorothy assured me he had never even imagined before—delighted him and he insisted that every-one, irrespective of what they were eating, should be accom-modated with freshly mixed mustard. The meal took longer than expected.

Two days in Wellington were largely devoted to political discussions with Mr. Nash and with other Ministers in his Government. These were a success—more successful, Mr. Nash later confessed to me, than he had expected. Some of his more extreme colleagues viewed with distaste the visit of this embodiment of Edwardian Toryism. They found it hard to rise above the party line, but they were soon disarmed by the strange charm of the man, his own statesmanlike approach to all problems and the vague look of uncomprehending idiocy if anyone tried to score a party point. In talking privately to Mr. Nash he made one very characteristic remark. He was giving advance information about the ill-fated Zeta. 'How does it work?' Mr. Nash asked. 'Well,' said Mr. Macmillan, looking vaguely about him, 'you just take sea water and turn it into power; and we are pretty good at sea water.' Mr. Nash told me later that he found it easier for a Labour Government in New

Zealand to deal with a Conservative rather than a Labour Government in the U.K. I suggested that this was a historic probability. The Conservative Party had always been the Party of Empire, while the Radicals and Socialists had in the past tended to be little Englanders. Mr. Holloway, the young Minister of Industries and Commerce, expressed himself, I believe, as dissatisfied with Mr. Macmillan's grasp of his subject. By his subject he meant his own—the details of New Zealand's industries and her industrial competitors in various parts of the world. Mr. Holloway, young, bright, intelligent, good-looking, blamed Mr. Macmillan's advisers for failing to brief him. I took a little sly pleasure in all this. Before Mr. Macmillan left London I had been ordered by the Commonwealth Relations Office to provide drafts of the speeches he would make on the major occasions. The Commonwealth Relations Office, it was explained, would provide him with briefs for the political discussions with New Zealand Ministers. I enquired, I hoped without ill-mannered asperity, whether it would not be better to reverse the roles. I had no idea, I said, what large international questions Mr. Macmillan wished to include in his speeches and even if I knew the questions I was not closely or fully aware of his views on them. On the other hand I was very well aware of the issues New Zealand Ministers wished to discuss and I thought I could advise, from my position of intimate and continuous contact, how these could be most profitably handled. What I had intended as a constructive and helpful suggestion was interpreted in the Commonwealth Relations Office as an example of a contradictory and insubordinate attitude and as an attempt to excuse myself from a difficult task.

The second half of the Macmillans' visit was spent in the South Island. In Dunedin Mr. Macmillan, proclaiming himself at home in a city so full of men of his own name, was relaxed and happy. He took great delight in starting a race for aged vintage cars and he enjoyed a visit to the albatross and the seals and a picnic tea on the beach with the Mayor, Sir Leonard Wright, and his family. On the Sunday we went to the Presbyterian Cathedral, where Mr. Macmillan was to read the lesson. We assembled in the hotel on the landing outside his room, waiting for him. He came out, and, looking vague and strained and a little cross, demanded of his private secretary, John Wyndham, 'Where is the lesson?' John Wyndham, looking ten times as vague as the Prime Minister and totally uncomprehending, turned hopelessly in our direction and enquired plaintively, 'Has anybody seen the lesson?' Somebody found it somewhere and all was well.

Mr. Macmillan, who had never quite thrown off his chill, decided he would take an afternoon's rest instead of attending the races where he was eagerly expected by a large crowd. The result was that when my wife and I arrived in an official car it was at once assumed that we were the Macmillans and our car was surrounded. It was quite clear as I got out that I was not Mr. Macmillan and indeed I modestly disclaimed such distinguished identity, calling out in self-deprecatory tones, 'I am not Mr. Macmillan, I am not Mr. Macmillan.' The whisper soon went round that it was only the British High Commissioner, whom a good many of them had seen before, and we pursued our way humbly and privately to the enclosure where my wife promptly had a welcome inspiration and backed a winning outsider.

From Dunedin we took our way back by road to Christchurch, calling at Timaru on the way. There Mr. Macmillan made a very good impromptu speech in the open-air Shell Theatre, carefully avoiding that sentimental message which had so much upset Lady Dorothy. Thereafter he mingled with the crowd in the brilliant sunlight and then hurried off secretly before an official lunch for a beer in the local with some tough types who did not know who he was. At Christchurch he made a speech on economic questions to a large gathering of business men and farmers. This was what they expected from him and they enjoyed it and got benefit from it; but he did not relish it at all and found it dull and heavy going. It was after dinner and like all civilised men he prefers not to be serious at that hour. The next day the whole party flew off to Australia and we embarked, a little flat and lonely, for Wellington in Mr. Nash's aeroplane. But our flatness and loneliness soon gave way to apprehension. As we approached Cook Strait the pilot reported that very low cloud at Paraparaumu, then the Wellington airport, would prevent us from landing and we should be obliged to go on to Ohakea, sixty miles further north and nearly a hundred miles from Wellington. Mr. Nash had an important Parliamentary engagement in Wellington and begged the pilot to make Paraparaumu if he possibly could. This the pilot dutifully and successfully did after what seemed to me—and also, as he later admitted, to him—a hair-raising flight low over the sea with the starboard wing tip, so it seemed, grazing the cliff face as we went and no sign whatever of the lofty Kapiti Island which stands sentinel at the approaches to the airfield. Mr. Nash was quite unperturbed.

Since that memorable and happy visit I have had little opportunity to see Mr. Macmillan. Later in my tour of duty as High Commissioner I felt his long-range impact very forcibly. We were in a difficult controversy with the New Zealand Government and I was in trouble, quite serious trouble, with Mr. Nash. He had made up his mind to take a step which from the point of view of the Commonwealth as a whole I thought rash and dangerous. I believed that if I could get rather more flexible instructions from London I could prevent him, but such instructions, I knew, could come only from the Prime Minister himself. They did come—in personal messages from him to me and in private letters from him to Mr. Nash. Wiser counsels prevailed. How this was achieved is a trade secret.

On my return to England at the end of 1959 I was made First
Civil Service Commissioner, responsible for the recruitment,
examination and selection of candidates for the Home Civil
and Foreign Services. As such I was deliberately removed as far
as possible from political influences and from the official point
of view Mr. Macmillan passed out of my life. Once during this
time I had half an hour, unpremeditated, unexpected, alone
with him. My wife and I had been bidden to an after-dinner
reception at Admiralty House (then the Prime Minister's home)
given in honour of some visiting President or potentate. It was
the usual glamorous crush—brilliant chandeliers, brilliant
jewels, some brilliant women, mostly rather seedy men in ill-
fitting tail-coats and white waistcoats. We swayed hither and
thither like a restless sea, drinking champagne and shouting
banalities to our acquaintances. Suddenly from this uneasy and
uncomfortable throng the Prime Minister himself led me away
to a couple of small gilt chairs at the end of a half-empty room,
and there we sat, ignoring the crowd, drinking and gossiping
together. My wife and my friends were somewhat astonished
at this mark of favour—if it was favour. What had I done, of
good or evil, to attract the Prime Minister's exclusive attention?
They would have been more astonished still if they had heard
our conversation—some reminiscent jokes about New Zealand
and then some talk about my present job. 'I enjoy it very much,'
I said, 'but I think I might do more.' 'What do you mean?' he
said. 'Do you think you ought to correct the exam papers
yourself?' 'No, certainly not,' I said, 'but I think I could help
you in some of your troubles. For example, why shouldn't I
run a competition for candidates for Bishoprics and Deaneries?'
Guildford was very much in the news at the time. He thought
it was splendid and better still when I suggested an open
competition for life peerages. 'Yes, yes,' he added gleefully,
'and why not for Ministerial jobs too? That would save me from
all these silly charges of nepotism.' And in that mood we

parted. We parted as we had met, with a kind of natural easy amity between us, and though I never really had much to do with him or gave him much help I have happy memories of him and admiration for his imperturbability, his civilised unconcern, his wit, his delight in good talk, good taste, good learning—all coupled, strangely and unexpectedly almost, with political sense and practical ability.

Some New Zealand
Prime Ministers

During my two and a half years in New Zealand I represented the views of my Government to no less than three New Zealand Prime Ministers. When I arrived in May 1957 Mr. Holland was still Prime Minister and remained so for a few more months, Mr. Holyoake succeeding him a short time before the General Election in November 1957. The National Party lost this election, and Mr. Nash, veteran leader of the Labour Party, precariously supported by a majority of one, became Prime Minister and remained so for the rest of my time.

I had seen Mr. Holland at a Commonwealth Prime Ministers' meeting in the United Kingdom in 1952, where he had disclosed a frank and vigorous good nature, and a somewhat hearty and uncomplicated approach to complex international tangles. On that occasion everyone had liked him. In the internal affairs of his own country he had enjoyed considerable success and was reported to have used great courage and determination to achieve it. He brought to the conference table at No. 10 a breezy confidence. He was jaunty. He bustled around, his square and burly figure supported on short and rapid legs. His large head and parrot face perked and smiled across the green baize table. He was what a New Zealander ought to be. I looked forward to close and continuous contacts with this friendly man.

When I reached New Zealand the decline in Mr. Holland's health, which led to his premature death in 1961, had in fact already begun. On the surface he seemed much the same. He could be gay and lively, and still at every dinner party, whether he was host or guest, he performed his conjuring tricks with the zest of an overgrown boy, delighting to remove your waist-coat without removing your coat, and so forth. At our first meeting at dinner he illustrated his stupendous catch of an immense marlin in the Bay of Islands by using my wife as the fish and landing her on the sofa with many hugs and pats. His talk and badinage flowed ceaselessly. But apart from the sustained social gusto there was clearly a weakening.

My first official contacts with him were unfortunate in the extreme. He got into his head that in one very important matter which concerned both the United Kingdom and New Zealand we had failed to consult him and keep him informed. This simply was not true. Nevertheless it would have been easy enough to bear the foolish reproaches which he directed at me personally—the inexperienced, ill-natured newcomer. The trouble was that he blurted out his irritation to the Press, and thus it became necessary for me to persuade him to contradict publicly the damaging and undeserved accusations which he had levelled at my Government. My subsequent official con-tacts with him were easier but not really very fruitful. He was trying to make up his mind to retire. He had bouts of ill-health of various kinds. But he hated the thought of handing over power to someone else and he feared that men were pointing at him and muttering, 'He is by no means what he was.' To a man of his buoyancy and vigour this was hard to endure and he sought to make up for it by a somewhat alienating vanity. It was not possible for me to discuss a subject of urgent importance with him or even to hand him a message from Mr. Macmillan without being first subjected to a twenty-minute monologue on his outstanding contribution to the revival of the National Party and his achievement as Prime Minister. Certainly his favourable judgment of himself was not undeserved, but it became an obsession with him and I must confess I did not altogether relish my frequent attendances upon him. All the same, the initial misunderstandings were quite forgotten and he was invariably friendly and jovial and confidential with me. In public he continued to speak with astonishing gusto, though it must often have cost him severe physical strain. His speeches, often impromptu, were remarkably fluent and humorous in a rather naive schoolboy manner. He was never dull to listen to, but there was an occasional error of taste which shocked and upset his friends. At the state luncheon given in honour of the retiring Governor-General Sir Willoughby Norrie, he included in his speech a remark on these lines: 'I have, of course, sent a report to the Queen about you, Your Excellency, and I don't think you would be altogether displeased if you could see what I wrote.' This piece of rather childish arrogance gave great offence. Who was Mr. Holland to report on the Governor-General and how could he have the impertinence to imply that it was in his power to confer favours?

His last few months as Prime Minister were rather trying for everyone, including himself. In spite of physical disability and a great deal of pain he clung to office and he finally devised a foolish and unworkable system by which he and Mr. Holyoake were to be, as it were, joint Prime Ministers—a sort of running-in period for Mr. Holyoake under close and experienced supervision. Poor Mr. Holyoake! His frustration must have been very great and his temper sorely tried. Nothing could have been more fatal to the conduct of business. Who was in charge?

Nobody knew, and so far as I was concerned I thought it prudent to deal separately with both Prime Ministers and hope to synthesise an answer of some sort. Fortunately this uncomfortable period was short and Mr. Holland's friends and advisers were at last able to persuade him that the state of his health required immediate and final retirement. Reluctantly he went, comforted with a G.C.B. as a reward for his great services to New Zealand. In retirement his health gradually improved and before I left New Zealand about two years later he was bobbish once more, often to be seen lunching at the Wellington Club, attending social functions and prepared once again to remove your waistcoat after dinner.

Mr. Holyoake's reign was very short and the greater part of his effort and attention in that time was inevitably concentrated on the General Election which was about to take place. He hardly had time to grasp the reins of office or to get himself involved in the wider Commonwealth and international affairs which were my main concern. In Mr. Holland's Government he had been a very successful Minister of Agriculture. Himself a farmer, he knew his subject well and was trusted and admired by the big farmers and the mighty producer boards, which are the most powerful lobby in New Zealand. In this capacity he had visited this country on many occasions to argue with us about the prices of dairy produce and meat and about rights of free entry.

I did not find it very easy at first to get to know Mr. Holyoake. He was friendly enough, but he seemed a trifle frigid and remote—an impression false and superficial and later dispelled by easy and agreeable contacts. I determined that as Mr. Holyoake was to be Prime Minister and might well be Prime Minister for the rest of my time in New Zealand, I must make a special effort to break down what seemed like reserve and establish some points of intimacy with him. Accordingly my wife and I arranged a quiet dinner party in our home for the Holyoakes and for another couple who had been exceptionally good to us since our arrival and who were intimate with them. It was to be a fruitful occasion and the best we could muster in the way of food and drink was expectantly prepared. But the evening was doomed to failure.

The chief catalyst, the male intermediary, arrived in a condition of fairly advanced intoxication and, I should guess, without the aid of his finely poised and intelligent wife, would not have arrived at all. The Holyoakes were late—we learnt to expect this—and from certain well-known sounds it was painfully clear to my wife and me that there had been serious dissension in the kitchen quarters. Somewhat uneasily we took our places at the table. The difficulties behind the scenes had apparently been resolved and we had a good dinner and some good wine. The conversation under my control was easy and agreeable enough—with Mrs. Holyoake and the female catalyst. At the other end of the table my wife fought a bold but losing battle with incoherent intemperance on her left and an elaborate politeness on her right. From time to time Mr. Holyoake's deep and golden tones could be heard expressing exceptional interest in the food, the wine, the weather, only to be interrupted and silenced by the staccato utterances which the man opposite him shot forth at breakneck speed and in incomprehensible terms. At my end of the table we hoped by conversational interchanges to make clear to each other that none of us had noticed anything at all out of the way.

At length the dinner ended, the table was cleared and the port and brandy and fruit were brought in. In accordance with normal custom the port went its round, and when it returned to me I was on the point of rising to my feet to propose 'The Queen'. I was only prevented by violent gesticulations from my wife, indicating to me that the male catalyst had no port in his glass. This was strange indeed. A minute before I had observed it full, but in that brief interim it had been drained off, no heel taps—my beautiful 1945 port brought over 14,000 miles of ocean and tended with such loving care. Once again I sent the decanter on its way and this time my wife, using vigorous methods, made clear what was expected—and at last we got the ceremony out of the way. But the evening never got going and the Holyoakes took their leave without any obvious signs of having enjoyed themselves or of wishing to get to know us any better—and indeed they had every reason to feel like that. The male catalyst hoped to spend another hour in a bibulous monologue in which one word alone, constantly reiterated, would have been comprehensible to anyone else—whisky. But his wife took charge and we were left to reflect upon our failure.

Mr. Holyoake's attitude to his duties as Prime Minister seemed casual, almost lazy; and one incident at the time, I must confess, gave me little confidence. A private message from Mr. Macmillan to Mr. Holyoake, to be delivered personally by me with certain explanations, arrived inconveniently but not abnormally one Sunday morning. Down to my office I went as I was obliged to decipher the message myself—not as difficult to the initiated as it sounds. With considerable trouble I obtained an appointment to see Mr. Holyoake at his private house at 2.30 p.m. I accordingly presented myself and rang the bell. I waited without result and rang again. It was hot and uncomfortable standing there. The door was wide open but I hardly liked to intrude and search through the rooms for the Prime Minister of New Zealand. I rang again. There was again no answer to the bell, but by chance somebody, I could hear, was beginning to descend the stairs, whistling lazily as he came. Mr. Holyoake came into view, large, relaxed, in shirt-sleeves. He noticed me with some surprise—a tiresome Sunday intruder —and enquired in rich golden tones if he could do anything for me. I explained that I had an appointment to see him in order to deliver a message from Mr. Macmillan. Disarmingly he said, 'To tell you the truth I had quite forgotten, but come in.'

The fact was, I suppose, that he was totally occupied with the election which he narrowly lost. I myself was surprised at some of his tactics, but then I hardly knew New Zealand and could not really judge whether they lost or gained him votes. His opponents, the Labour Party, were in the habit of deriding the National Party as the party of the rich, the well-to-do, the snobs, the well-educated, the intellectuals—a feeble sort of propaganda which long since lost all its edge in this country. Mr. Holyoake saw fit to make a spirited reply, declaring with pride that he was no intellectual, he was not well educated; he had left school when he was fourteen and had never been near a university. The inference was that he, therefore, was peculiarly well qualified to be Prime Minister of New Zealand. At any rate he failed to convince the electorate, and the Labour Party, under Mr. Nash, were returned with an effective majority of one in a house of eighty.

Mr. Nash was a very different type. In a sense he was a professional politician and had been for a very long time. He had served with distinction in Peter Fraser's war-time Government and had represented the interests of New Zealand in both Washington and London at different times during the war. He was known to a number of Commonwealth and European politicians and he had a profound interest in international problems. Alone among New Zealand politicians of that time he had some pretensions to being a world figure. Although by no calculation could New Zealand have been regarded as a great or important Power, Mr. Nash spoke with authority and other world statesmen were ready to listen; his views were well informed and liberal and, although occasionally he seemed to be lost in visionary speculations, he arrived in the end at a practical, hard-headed and courageous attitude. Nearly all New Zealanders, whatever their party, were proud to have Mr. Nash representing them overseas.

At home it was a very different matter. Mr. Nash was an old-time Labour politician brought up in the Labour movement in this country and patiently devoted to the Fabian principles which he had imbibed before emigrating to New Zealand. His early life he spent in Kidderminster and he did not set out for New Zealand before he was nearly thirty. This had some interesting consequences. His socialism was old-fashioned. He clung to Fabian doctrine as New Zealand women cling to the modes and manners of their emigrating grandmothers. He was intensely devoted to Britain—as he always called it. His affection was direct, personal, local. He and the Governor-General of the time, Lord Cobham, passed happy hours together in reminiscences of Worcestershire. Nearly all New Zealanders are loyally devoted to 'the old country' and the Crown. This is a very strong feeling, but it draws its strength from tradition and does not grow, as it were, direct from English soil. Mr. Holyoake, for example, came of a family which had been settled in New Zealand for more than a hundred years and his attitude to Britain, though understanding, considerate and loyally attached, was naturally less tender, less compassionate. There is an interesting distinction here. Mr. Holyoake, like all long-settled and well-established New Zealanders, could quickly take offence at what seemed to him —and sometimes rightly so—patronising affronts from cock-sure Englishmen. Most New Zealanders are a little prickly and it is easy to see why. Mr. Nash's attitude to this sort of thing was totally different. If he felt that the British Government or some visiting Englishman had behaved with superior arrogance he would be grieved and unhappy—not affronted—upset, as any man is by the ill-behaviour of his own family. Disputes between the two countries, which, of course, arose from time to time, were a personal worry and distress to him, but when he had taken his position he fought as an equal and made no cringing concession whatever to superior power. And when the quarrel was all over the affection was deeper than ever.

New Zealanders themselves may have been subconsciously aware of this difference of approach. They never quite knew where they had Mr. Nash. Was he one of them or was he still, if you scratched below the surface, just another Pommy? Certainly he never exchanged his Worcestershire accent for the very individual New Zealand version of our language. But on the whole he was a popular man, admired by all for his international repute, liked by thousands who had first-hand experience of his charm and kindness, mistrusted by some who thought him the prisoner of class hatred (which he certainly was not). He had been Finance Minister in Peter Fraser's Government and he was inclined to fancy his skill in manipulating fiscal policies. Some of these, inevitably in the hands of an old-fashioned Fabian, had borne hard upon the well-to-do, who were, in general but by no means universally, alienated from him. To his political colleagues and to his officials his most irritating quality was his insistence upon centralisation and his limitless powers of procrastination. Nothing could be decided without him and with him nothing could be decided quickly.

For my part I was immediately taken with this man. He had style and quality and immense courage and tenacity. Squat and foursquare he stumped boldly through life, indefatigable, talkative to the point of tedium, but always saved by a touch of humour or a visitation of grace. He was close on eighty when he became Prime Minister, but age meant nothing to him. He was determined to make the most of his great office. He loved the power and influence it brought him and he loved still more the wider personal contacts, the visiting politicians, the politicians overseas—he was an unwearied and inveterate traveller—and his own countrymen, of every party and profession, up and down New Zealand. He missed nothing. The annual dinner of the local rugby team was to him as interesting and exciting as a state banquet for the Queen Mother, and he gave himself equally and tirelessly to both, talking on, reminiscing, holding the floor, while men of half his age prayed in silence for their beds.

The making of speeches was the breath of life to him. He rarely had time to prepare them, but when he did, when he took pains to harness his thoughts and images, he could speak very well. Even his unprepared speeches were not dull, though they were often absurdly protracted. He was constantly playing for time, using long and meaningless prepositional phrases, like 'associated with' and 'in connection with' and 'in relation to', inserting long irrelevant words—his favourite was 'inferentially'—in the hopes that while they were falling heedlessly from his lips some bright thought would come to him and light up and enliven the whole speech. And it usually did. But having thus groped his way to a fleeting success he felt encouraged to go on and on. In these unprepared orations he never had any idea how he would bring them to an end, so that he seemed like a man continually fumbling for his tail and never finding it. Once I remember hearing him welcome, at some reception, a visiting football team from Fiji. He was largely unprepared, but he managed rather well; he liked this sort of occasion. Again he could not finish. Those of us who knew him well were quite aware that he was in the usual predicament and that we might have to wait a considerable time, but none of us was prepared to see him carried away by a spontaneous invention which seemed to be self-perpetuating. 'Hairemai, hairemai, hairemai,' he said. 'The greeting given by the eloquent Maori race, whose contribution to the civilization of New Zealand and those associated with it should never be forgotten in connection with their history. Hairemai, hairemai, hairemai—Welcome, welcome, welcome. Thrice welcome—or, as the Maoris say, Hairemai, hairemai, hairemai—which, etc., etc. . . .'

If I laugh at these shifts and stratagems I do not despise them. Mr. Nash conceived his duty as Prime Minister as a combination of Gladstone and John Wesley. I was bold enough—bold

F

through his confidence and affection—to tell him that he must
relax and relent in some directions, that the Bata Shoe Company could survive without his welcome intrusion into their
annual dinner, that the social evenings with various societies and
clubs in the Lower Hutt would not resent his absence, the great
man of New Zealand. He could have spared himself all this, but
he would not. It was his strength and his weakness. More and
more New Zealanders became aware of the stocky figure with
white hair, firm and amiable expression and shabby clothes,
who exuded good nature and Christian companionship, who
spoke to them, at length, but with obvious friendliness and
good humour. Was this King Dick Seddon come to life again?
On the other hand, his in-tray became very full. His colleagues
and his official advisers waited not very hopefully for his
decisions.

It was possible to entice him away from his duty in Parliament and from his innumerable social occasions. It was infrequently possible, and when he came to my house he was at
ease and charming and relaxed. One night we arranged to have
a *partie carré*—my wife and I and Mr. and Mrs. Nash. It was a
great success. We dined well and Mr. Nash relished every wine
that the traditional customs of my country offered him. He and
I were left in intimate isolation with our port and brandy.
When we had satisfied ourselves we began our progress to my
wife's sitting-room, passing on our way my billiard-room, at
that time of year cold and mainly unused. He was eager to have
a game of snooker. He did not mind the cold; there would be
time for a hundred up at least before we joined the ladies. I
demurred; it was late, it was very cold and he was tired (so
indeed was I!). Reluctantly he gave way. Subsequently I learnt
that he was a very good snooker-player. He would have been
glad to demonstrate the skill of Old England against what he
considered as New England.

Mr. Nash used to claim that he needed no more than four

hours' sleep. This was no doubt true, but he found it hard to understand or excuse the weak and slothful habits of more ordinary mortals. If Parliament sat late, he, of course, sat late in it. He was Leader of the House and, moreover, he had a majority of only one, so that the Whips were severe even with the Prime Minister. If Parliament was not sitting he worked in his room until all hours. The middle of the night was about the only time he was undisturbed and could dispose of some files, which had been waiting so long for his attention. In the daytime he was besieged by callers. Everyone had to be seen. He made himself absurdly accessible to every Tom, Dick and Harry, so that Cabinet Ministers, High Commissioners, Ambassadors and high officials often had to wait in the queue. But his private secretaries were very good and had a much better judgment of priorities than their master. They managed him well and he also had the unselfish and continuous support of his chief official Alister McIntosh. He sometimes deplored the long hours and dilatory habits of his master, but he was fond of him and anxious always to help him and spare him worry and fatigue. Mr. Nash understood very clearly the workings of democracy in New Zealand. No New Zealand Minister would dare to fence himself off from the close approach of the public. He was but one of them, with no particular title to their consideration. He wished to mix on easy and hearty terms with all and sundry. That was the way Dick Seddon had behaved; that was the way to popularity and power. Some of his Cabinet colleagues grew restive with him. He over-centralised, he insisted on being consulted on almost everything and then he delayed giving his opinion. At Cabinet he was wordy and inconclusive. They had a good deal to put up with, but then he was very experienced, much more experienced than any of them, and his public relations were much more firmly and soundly based. He thought deeper than any of them and generally spoke better if a little longer. All New Zealand politicians run to inordinate length.

He was unquestionably the leader and if he had died suddenly
—which at certain times of strain appeared not at all improbable
—there would have been a disputed succession and the Labour
Party would have lost the next election without any question
at all. In fact they did so even under Mr. Nash's leadership. I
count myself fortunate to have known him so intimately at a
time when he, though far past the prime of life, achieved his
highest ambition and pulled out every stop he had to make the
most of it, to enjoy it to the top of his bent and to do his utmost
duty unsparingly and untiringly. That is Man at his best.

2

The Gods of War

IN 1957 Hutchinson published a book by Major-General Sir John Kennedy entitled *The Business of War*. The book was not to everybody's taste. General Kennedy was a comparatively unknown officer who had held no command during the war. He had, it was generally admitted by those who knew, carried out his duties as Director of Military Operations at the War Office with great ability and attention to duty. But other officers of the same rank, in the Army and in the other two Services, had made equally notable contributions. Why should the D.M.O. assume that he was better qualified than they to explain the 'business of war'? Besides he had so organised and arranged his book, he had so distributed the emphasis, as to make it appear that his was the master strategic mind, that all the sound and wise plans had been conceived and advocated by him—sometimes, it appeared, in a sort of Socratic dialogue with the C.I.G.S., in which the D.M.O., like Socrates, was invariably triumphant. It is true that the book has curious omissions. It is only in the preface by Brigadier Sir Bernard Fergusson that the inter-Service planning staffs receive any mention at all. Occasional reference is made to the work of the General Staff in the War Office, but the main impression left on the readers'

mind is that the true strategy was made by Kennedy with a
little help from Brooke. This is so much the case that the ill-
disposed have suggested that the alternative title to the book
ought to be—'I and the C.I.G.S.'.

For my part I thought the book rather good, even if it
occasionally overreaches itself. I thought it good because it
presents the issues clearly and the opinions expressed are
generally soundly based. I thought it good because I know from
first-hand experience that General Kennedy was a very good
D.M.O. I found it especially interesting because it was the
work of a somewhat remote and enigmatic character who
ordered my life and the life of some of my closest friends for a
year or two at the beginning of the war while we were on the
General Staff at the War Office. At the time we had a sort of
feeling that if he was aware of us at all he was hostile and
oppressive. We thought it more likely that he had not noticed
us—and this impression is confirmed by his book, where not
even his tireless, faithful deputy, Brigadier Frank Simpson, gets
a single mention—but because we were unwilling to admit our
insignificance we built our theories about him on the assumption that he was in fact hostile and oppressive. In those days he
was the nearest approach to a 'war leader' that we knew. I have
recorded in another chapter my own encounter with the
Prime Minister on the telephone, but that was exceptional.
From day to day General Kennedy stalked along those grim
passages, tall and gangling, with knees and feet turning out-
wards at an exaggerated angle. He was our great leader, continuously demanding and exacting. It amused us to mitigate
our sometimes painful sentence by making up stories about him.
To us he was a bird of ill-omen. If you did not detect his
onward approach and if you failed to escape down a side
passage you were certain, we pretended, to receive a stinging
reproach for neglect or a peremptory order to produce at once
some information which you had not got. He was an incubus,

something you could not shake off. He was with you day and night, tormenting you. He followed you home, he put stones in your shoes, he altered the trains and sent you off to unwanted destinations. He never left you alone. He waited in hiding in the dark of his outer office to pounce out upon you as you passed along the passage at the end of a wearying day. It was much safer we found to make a long detour to avoid his door and to go out at a different exit. But he soon got wise to that and as you approached this exit to freedom, by remote control from his room he slammed it in your face. There seemed no limit to his powers.

Dear D.M.O., unwittingly you provided us with great amusement and some lightening of the burden of our work. If you ever read this nonsense I do not think it will make you laugh, but you need not be annoyed. We admired you very much. We preened ourselves if ever you praised us and you were the kind of man who exacts and deserves good service. We knew how overburdened you were and we did not really expect that you could have time or energy for personal contacts with us. Once late at night in your room, hammering at some problem, I made you laugh. I made an excuse half an hour later to come back to see you, so that I might follow up my success and let off another joke. It misfired badly and I was summarily ejected, to the intense merriment of my colleagues.

Apart from the constant fear and overhanging shadow of General Kennedy we did not often come within the touch of the seats of power. Once I was sent to see the new V.C.I.G.S.—Lieutenant-General Sir A. Nye—to explain some problem on which I was supposed to be the local expert. He was a good prober and his somewhat frigid and forbidding manner made the occasion more alarming than it need have been. That was my first encounter with him. I saw him many times thereafter sitting in committee with the other Vice-Chiefs and occasionally if Brooke was away with the big Chiefs themselves. He was always on the spot, as well briefed as he was well groomed, as conscious of his brisk efficiency as he was of his good looks, firm in opinion, intolerant, with something of a lawyer's disputatious self-confidence. One head-on clash with the First Sea Lord, Andrew Cunningham, has remained clear in my memory. It was at a Chiefs of Staff meeting at which Nye was deputising for Brooke. On a question of rather complicated detail and of no great strategic interest there was a direct contradiction on a matter of fact between the War Office and the Admiralty briefs. Nye gave out, in his usual clipped and confident style, the facts and the solution—an admirable, lucid exposition intended to deal summarily with this unimportant matter without further question. Nye was too sure of himself to notice the storm gathering in the red-hot countenance of the First Sea Lord and was, therefore, quite unprepared for the blast of contradiction which immediately assailed him. I have no doubt that the somewhat irascible Cunningham, irritated by the smug assurance of a comparatively junior officer, was tempted beyond his brief and said more perhaps than the facts would support. When the storm died out, Nye, also red in the face, but poker-straight and collected as ever, replied in maddeningly unctuous tones, 'First Sea Lord, you impugn both my memory and my veracity—two qualities on which I am inclined to pride myself.' The intervention of the Chief of the Air Staff, Portal, who was in the chair, prevented any further unmannerly display and the matter was postponed so that the facts might be established. Later in life I was indebted to Nye for a useful piece of worldly advice. It was just before I left for New Zealand to be High Commissioner and he and his wife were having a quiet dinner with us in our London house. 'At your official dinner parties,' he admonished me, 'see that after dinner the senior lady is put next to the most boring male guest. This will ensure that your party packs up in good time.'

One night when I was working late in the War Office—as indeed everyone often did—there came a call from my brother, who was then Deputy D.M.O. The Secretary of State, then David Margesson, was anxious to learn something detailed and particular about one of my problems—Syria, I think. Would I please go along to his room and give him the necessary information? It was late—11 p.m. perhaps—and he, I am sure, was very very tired. I was nervous. I had had no assignment of this kind before and I knew nothing whatever about the Secretary of State except that he had been a very successful and disciplinary Chief Whip, with all the qualities of an admirable school prefect. He was totally different from anything I had expected. He bade me sit down, he was friendly, charming, attentive. He completed his inquisition, to which I replied to the best of my ability. He was appreciative, sympathetic about the time of night, and immediately offered me a whisky and soda—unknown delight, unexpected attention in this impersonal place and these austere times. We chatted in easy sympathy and parted—the great Secretary of State and the temporary General Staff Officer II. It made a deep impression on me, which has remained. One more session with him I experienced. Lord Wedgwood was introducing some motion in the House of Lords—again I think it was the Syrian campaign or the aftermath, the position of the Jews or something of the kind. Margesson treated the question lightly, in a somewhat chaffing spirit. He knew Josh Wedgwood. He handled him well, and I, who had thought the question awkward and dangerous, was left wondering at his political skill. Poor David Margesson, he had been too good a whipper-in for Chamberlain and it cannot have surprised him very much that he was shortly kicked upstairs. The blow, I have always heard, was very sudden, quite unheralded and rather unceremonious. Mr. Macmillan was not the first Prime Minister to favour the swift and sudden disposal of his victims.

During the grim days of the Battle of Crete I had some further rather closer experience of the exercise of authority in war. Brigadier Vivian Dykes, then Director of Plans in the War Office, plucked me out of my room one morning and carried me off with him to a meeting in the Air Ministry. Air Marshal Sir Arthur Harris, then Vice-Chief of Air Staff, was in the Chair, Vivian Dykes and I represented the War Office and Air Commodore Coryton was also present. The Prime Minister, Harris explained, wished the War Office to send a telegram to Wavell about the situation in Crete—as if we were not sending and receiving telegrams on this subject at every hour of the day and night. The Prime Minister was not satisfied with the conduct of operations—he never was—and he wished certain suggestions to be put to the Commander-in-Chief. As Harris started to read from his notes what these suggestions were, our consternation increased. How could we fight this battle from Whitehall? Wavell had no doubt considered all these things. It was wrong to harass him, to make him feel a lack of confidence at home. In the midst of this painfully embarrassing recital by Harris, Coryton, who shared our misgivings and disquiet, looked across the table at us, tapping his head and jerking it towards Harris to indicate the mental derangement in high places. This gesture, which delighted us, was observed by Harris, who happened to look up suddenly from his notes, and Coryton, like any truant schoolboy, hastily pretended that he was rubbing some skin irritation on his forehead. This was a little light relief at a sombre time. Dykes and I retired to the War Office and not for the last time I tried to devise a form of words which would serve to give effect to the Prime Minister's wishes without causing Wavell to offer his resignation.

Wavell himself I had at this time never seen, but my job on the General Staff brought me close not only to his problems but to his manner of handling them. I saw his appreciations, and sometimes, if my job really required it, some of his personal telegrams to the C.I.G.S. Moreover, my brother, who had accompanied Anthony Eden and the C.I.G.S., then Sir John Dill, to the Middle East before the Greek campaign, had seen Wavell at work, had worked for him, knew him indeed quite well; and all that he told me increased my admiration for this strangely taciturn soldier, who wrote like an angel and hardly spoke at all. My brother described to me a meeting in Cairo with Mr. Eden, the Commanders-in-Chief, the C.I.G.S. and the full panoply—great argument about it and about, lengthy and often pointless disputation, and Wavell silent, withdrawn, now and again rising from his chair and going across the room apparently to examine the books in his bookcase, hoping no doubt to draw more inspiration from their silence than he could from the continuous loquacity around him. Finally when argument had spent itself he fixed the company with his single eye and gave out the answer, the policy, the plan, with notable economy of words and directness of style. The terrible disasters of Greece and Crete and the Western Desert had not yet assailed this strong and long-suffering man. His victories over the Italians in Cyrenaica and in Eritrea and Ethiopia—our first victories in the war—had raised him to such a point of popular acclaim that once, when, in London at about this time, he chanced to go to a theatre, the audience spotted him and spontaneously applauded his presence.

I myself never set eyes on him until after he had passed through the agonies and frustrations of defeat in the Middle East and defeat in the Far East. But I had in fact had a letter from him, strange and unexpected reward for my loyal admiration. One dull afternoon in, I think, August 1942 when I, by this time a G.S.O. II in the Joint Planning Staff in the War Cabinet Office, was supposed to be writing a strategic apprecia- tion on a most improbable, unimportant, hypothetical issue, I was seized by frustration and despair. Why were we not doing better? Why did we waste time and energy on irrelevant

futilities? Why did we not go to the root of the matter? We
were hanging back, unwilling to make sacrifices. The mood of
1940 seemed to have left us and perhaps the inspiring leadership
of those days had a little lost its savour. The 'V' sign and the
eternal cigar seemed inappropriate symbols when all that was
needed was stern, unbending, austere, Puritanical devotion. In
my perhaps somewhat self-conscious despair I started to write,
on the back of my dull regimented appreciation, an open letter
to Wavell. Was he not a second Oliver, a commander, if ever
there was one, 'Who knows what he fights for and loves what
he knows?' While thus absorbed, Joan Bright, now Mrs. Joan
Astley, and at that time General Ismay's personal assistant,
chanced to come into my room. What was I about? she asked.
'An appreciation,' I replied, 'a rather dull and pointless strategic
appreciation.' 'You look rather animated,' she said; and
gradually, because she is a sympathetic person, she discovered
what I really was about. She snatched it up and read it, fell in
with my mood, declared that Wavell, whom she knew well,
would be interested and responsive, and to my surprise and
not, I confess, entirely against my wishes, said she would send it
to him as from an anonymous G.II—and so she did. This letter
I did not see again for twenty years and, though I remembered
the gist of it, I had forgotten its rather vigorous and radical
style. I give it here in the form in which it was sent. It is clearly
unfinished but it was enough to stimulate Wavell into a reply
of deep historical importance.

Dear General Wavell,
    We work, some of us because we have to and some
because we really want to contribute to victory. Some of us
pray—in fear and anxiety or from habit; few from burning
faith. We all grumble and grow weary; some of us because
we want to have the war over, not because we want to beat
our enemies and prove that we are Englishmen; some of us

because we are ashamed of what is happening to Russia, and would make a rash and generous sacrifice. Some of us still lift longing eyes to a new heaven and a new earth, here in our country, and will fight for a distant ideal. Others will struggle with inhuman bitterness to retain what they have got and would make peace with our enemies if that would give them their dirty security. As many motives as there are men: and their only unity is discontent.

We are all dissatisfied with the direction of the War. We blame the Prime Minister, the Press, the Archbishops, the Chiefs of Staff, the House of Commons, Admirals, Coal-miners, Generals, Mr. Shinwell, Pacifists, the War Office—anything and anybody, you see, to give vent to our spleen. Nothing is perfect; all these persons and things could of course be better, but that wouldn't rouse England to win the War and save herself and Europe.

There was once a very great Englishman who knew what he fought for and loved what he knew. He had a vast courage and humanity and a profound unswerving faith. But he was no dreamer. By his own exertions he trained the best army in Europe and with this instrument he swept away his vain, deluded and divided opponents. You remember how he used to say 'Put your trust in God and keep your powder dry'.

We are beginning to get plenty of powder but where shall we find a God to trust in?

You have won victories, you have suffered defeats. We wish to dissect neither. What we are interested in is your hidden power which has made you the strong rock of our confidence. If that power comes from a strong faith in your God, come and help our unbelief.

You shall have what instruments you want, you shall have our rights and liberties, if you will raise us up again and help us to defeat our enemies. You can lock up the doors of the

House of Commons and take away that shining bauble; you
can have what advisers you choose; you can deny us food,
drink, amusements, if it suits your all embracing purpose.
We know that when we have proved ourselves a restored
and noble people and have led the world to victory over
iniquity, we shall have won back our independence and you
your release from the heaviest burden Destiny can impose.

Wavell's reply has already been included in part in his
biography by John Connell. I was anxious, nevertheless, to
include it in my recollections of this great man and I am indebted to Wavell's executors for their permission to produce
it here.

New Delhi,
11th September, 1942

My dear G.II,

I have read the letter you sent me by Joan Bright. You
seem to have discovered the main ethical objection to war
for intelligent people, that it is so deplorably dull and usually
so inefficiently run. 'I see no reason why the human race, so
inefficient in matters of peace, should suddenly become
efficient in time of War.' I've forgotten where I saw that but
it has always seemed to me that most people seeing the
muddles of war forget the muddles of peace and the general
inefficiency of the human race in ordering its affairs. War is
a wasteful, boring, muddled affair; and the people of fine
intelligence (which I assume you to be) either resign themselves to it or fret badly, especially if they are near the heart
of things and can see matters which ought to be done, or
done better, and cannot contrive to get them set right. Isn't
something like that the root of your discontent?

As to leadership. Cromwell, as you say, was a very great
Englishman, a common-sense country gentleman with a gift

of simple direct speech, who had great faith, who saw things were wrong and set himself to put them right. I believe his faith was in England rather than in the particular brand of government preached by his Puritans. I don't think he really approved of that: England certainly didn't and got rid of Puritanism as soon as possible after his death. I don't think he roused all England, only quite a small part of it. He raised a very efficient but very small army of picked men.

Isn't Lincoln an even better example of what we want today—wise, simple, with far-reaching vision, great faith and enduring courage? 'The Last of the Kings' John Buchan called him, I think, in one of his tales, thinking I suppose of Carlyle's *Heroes and Hero-Worship* (I haven't read it for many years but remember something of his Hero as a King).

But is there really anything very wrong with our leadership today, can you find a man to lead us with greater courage, greater faith in England, more power of inspiration than the P.M.? He has made mistakes, he will make a good many more, he is difficult in many ways; but taking it by and large I don't think our general strategy has been bad, given our resources; I should say, though I know less of it, that our diplomacy has been adequate on the whole; and we have certainly had resolute courageous confident leadership at the head. I don't think in this imperfect world we can hope for more at the present, and I believe that 'Winston duce et auspice Winston' we shall come through all right. *After* the war I should advise the removal from high places of everyone over say fifty if possible, and that the New Model for peace should be made by the young or comparatively young men. I dare say they will make little better of it, but it will be the world they have to live in; we old men shall only have to die in it.

Myself (since you have mentioned me as a White Hope)— quite small light table beer, I am afraid; a good journeyman

soldier who knows his job reasonably well, not afraid of
responsibility but not seeking it; quite intelligent for one of
the Unintelligentsia; confident enough in his normal judgment of things military, but no divine fire for leadership of a
people. So that's that.

Yours,
Wavell

He happened to be in London later that year. Joan Bright had
been asked to a cocktail party at Chips Channon's house in Bel-
grave Square at which Wavell was to be the lion. Joan asked
Chips if I might come too, and so I had my first encounter with
Wavell. So far as I remember it, it was a smart sort of party—
smart for those days, at any rate—in a large room in a large house.
There was the usual cocktail-party chatter and noise, the usual
screaming of banalities, the usual restless surge from one part
of the room to another. Wavell was set apart from the surge,
placed in position at the end of the room by the window, and
different guests were from time to time discreetly led up and
introduced to him—inevitable but artificial arrangement which
freezes all conversation at its source, especially as it was, on this
occasion, up to Wavell to choose the topic and he would far
rather have remained silent. It was some time before I was
pushed into the shy and taciturn presence and in the interim my
most interesting conversation was with Wavell's two sisters.
These two placid, natural, unassuming, well-bred, middle-aged
English ladies seemed to have no affinity with their smart
surroundings, and yet their good breeding kept them from
looking out of place. On the contrary their modest demeanour
and appearance made everything else in that glittering room
seem a little extravagant, a little tawdry, a little overdone.
Quietly they moved about together, keeping to the wall and
the less conspicuous corners of the room. They spoke of their
famous brother with an engaging affection and admiration. He

was about to publish, they told me, the second volume of his life of Allenby and later on an anthology of all the English poetry he knew by heart. It was surprising, they said, how much poetry he did know. It was the effort of memory, I felt, which excited their admiration, rather than the conjunction in this rugged, masculine, overburdened soldier of the poetic and the military art. How, in such exacting circumstances, did he find time and nervous energy? I mused aloud, only to be answered by the enunciation of one of those principles which have always guided this class of English people. 'Of course,' one of the Miss Wavells said, 'of course, it is always possible to find time for anything important.'

From this unexpected encounter—unexpected in these rich and worldly surroundings—I was led up to the fringes of the presence. Poor Wavell—he certainly hated this sort of occasion. He was uncomfortable, ill at ease, more taciturn than ever, and the Indian lady, who was conducting a unilateral conversation with him about what was to her, no doubt, a subject of consuming interest, was manifestly making no headway at all. After hovering uncomfortably and, as it seemed to me, conspicuously at his outskirts, I was formally introduced. Hearing my name he cast a glance upon me from his single eye, and looking away again said that my brother was well and doing his job effectively. The voice was thicker than I had expected, not bell-like and no deep tones. His single glance had seemed almost baleful, certainly uninterested, as if it were a man giving you but half his attention and that not steadily. His face was much lined and puckered, tending to heaviness about the jowl, his neck thick, his stature short. Yet about him was an air of indefinable distinction and in his silence you could feel the latent power of the man. His manner was a trifle perfunctory, not unfriendly but not warm or welcoming. I had my very short innings and was then moved on. Later he perambulated less formally, less officially, amongst groups of guests and I had

G

a further word or two. He was impressive and yet at this period of time—after the crushing burden of the Middle East Command and the early disasters of the Japanese war—it was not surprising that he should seem a little lacking in motive power, fagged and tired, dispirited, as if he saw everything ending in the nothing all things end in. There was certainly none of the punch and gusto of Churchill. Perhaps, after all, his own estimate of himself was nearer the truth than my wishful thinking.

In 1943 I was made Secretary of the Joint Planning Staff. As such I became a member of the Military Secretariat of the War Cabinet with General Ismay as my Chief. In this very central position I saw a good many high-ranking officers, some already at the top and some very clearly on the way up. The three Directors of Plans, Army, Navy and Air Force, who together with their inter-Service staff formed the Joint Planning Staff, were my immediate concern and my daily and hourly masters. The Directors themselves were hand-picked officers at Brigadier level and all whom I served rose later to exalted rank and great responsibility, as did many at the more junior levels.

Of my Chief, General Ismay, the world has heard much and he himself has left a wise and measured account of the endless discussions and difficult decisions in which he played such an individual part. He is a cheerful, friendly man, a lover of good living, anxious always and in all circumstances to feel that 'all is for the best in the best of all possible worlds', agreeable and smiling to all and sundry, warm and affectionate, not in the least degree ingratiating but determined to promote harmony, to make sure that there is no unnecessary grit in the machine. He could be critical and reproachful if he thought that you were making unnecessary grit, doing something to generate disharmony. Once, I remember very clearly, he sent for me on a Sunday morning. He had been reading a paper by the Joint Planning Staff which he disliked very much. Was not a member

of his staff the Secretary of this body? How could he let such
turgid stuff be submitted to the Chiefs of Staff? He sent for me
at once and gave me a very painful and very wounding reproof.
I was also, I explained, the servant of the Directors of Plans. I
could not write things which they would not approve and
sign. Of course not, of course not—but the form in which these
foolish opinions were presented was my affair, he objected. The
views might be nonsense but at least, if I did my job properly,
they could be readable, and if they had that quality it would
take some of the ill-tempered sting out of the inevitable
criticism. Time and tempers would be spared and disharmony
would not prevail. He was right, of course, and I learnt an
important lesson from his reproof. He tried to drive it home,
which he need not have done, by proceeding to show me, not
without some manifestations of false modesty, an appreciation
he had written, years before, at the Staff College. I suppose that
the Directing Staff had praised it highly and he had preserved
it, just as many of us preserve the good reports of our schoolmasters. He produced it and read and emphasised certain parts
of it. I was less impressed by this venial flirtation with vanity
than I had been by the first impact of the direct rocket. I retired
ruffled and upset because I knew I had done badly and because,
in spite of my irritation with his method of reproof, I knew
that I very much valued his good opinion. I went back to my
own office. There was plenty to do. I was soon immersed in
some other critical problem, when the phone rang. General
Ismay was on the phone. Would I lunch with him at White's?
Of course I did and enjoyed it immensely. This little, unimportant episode is so characteristic that I recount it. He would
never let the sun go down upon his wrath; and that in all his
dealings was his great strength.

His life during the war was anything but tranquil, but he
does not look for tranquillity, does not much like it. He is
always busy and bustling, so eager and alert that he hardly

seems to be listening, and yet he was the confidant of most Commanders-in-Chief and many Ministers, always ready with wise and soothing advice. Few temperaments could have remained steady and good-humoured in such twisting and torturing circumstances. It was as if he were living a large part of his life in a badminton court in which the Prime Minister was locked in violent combat with the Chiefs of Staff and he was the shuttlecock, constantly beaten backwards and forwards with immoderate imprecations from one to the other. But it was a very stiff and splendid game which could never have been played at all if there had been no smiling, pug-like, willing shuttlecock.

The lack of sleep, the exacting and unreasonable demands, the strain of constantly searching for solutions, constructing bridges on which conflicting minds could meet, exploring escape routes from an overpowering impasse, manufacturing consolations for angry and frustrated Commanders—all this took its toll. I have seen General Ismay near the end of his tether, ill and exhausted, but his powers of recovery and his sense of duty were very strong. He was soon back in the fight. Sometimes, not surprisingly, in moments of fatigue there was a slowness and hesitation about his processes of thought. It was not a happy experience, at the end of a very late meeting, to find oneself summoned to the General's room to 'help' in drafting a telegram which the meeting, just concluded, had decided must be sent that night to some Commanders-in-Chief or to the United States Chiefs of Staff, or maybe to the President himself. He would send for a shorthand-writer and begin with many false starts to dictate the message, begging us at the same time to interrupt if he was missing a point or giving a wrong emphasis. This was something that could not sensibly be done, for we had no idea what he had in mind for the beginning, middle and end of his message. If, through apprehension that some crucial point was being lost, we made an interjection, it merely added to the general confusion. 'Oh yes, of course,' he would say. 'Wait a minute. Where was I? What?' And the poor shorthand-writer would begin to read back, but before one sentence was uttered he would be off again. 'Oh! I think "induce" rather than "persuade". What? And what was your thought? Yes, well how shall we put it? What?' And before you could frame it in words he had another bright idea and back we went to the beginning again. How the shorthand-writer produced anything at all passed my comprehension. These were painful sessions and it is a bad way to work—far better to let the junior officer produce a draft and then correct and improve it in silence and alone.

I do not think that General Ismay very much liked being alone. He wants company, men to talk to, men to listen to his stories. He has plenty of ideas and was by no means lacking in imagination, but as the ideas and images flow into his head he must immediately find an audience to try them on. He is not reflective or meditative by nature. Well do I remember a period during which he was engaged in composing a speech of great moment to be delivered to an American audience. This continuously occupied his mind, but there were no long and silent sessions of lonely composition. As soon as a short section, a few sentences, had formed themselves in his head he must find a friend and give him a drink and try the eloquence on him. I was much in his way at this time. He duly delivered the speech, but I never bothered to read it; I had heard so much of it so often.

I think my most treasured recollection of this lovable man is of an encounter with him in a passage in the War Cabinet Offices. I was hurrying on my way, busy, preoccupied, concentrated, carrying a telegram, fetching a report, doing something urgent—that was the usual state of mind—when I ran into my General. 'Where are you going, George?' he said. 'I am rushing a report into the Chiefs of Staff Secretariat,' I said, or something of the kind. 'But you mustn't,' he said, 'you are suspended from duty.' For a moment I had an uncomfortable feeling, a hasty recapitulation of culpable negligences, but he was smiling, his pug-like wrinkles upward-turning, his eyes merry. 'What do you mean, sir?' I asked. 'The Prime Minister,' he said, 'has seen a report by one of the staffs to which he takes great exception. It should never have been written, let alone circulated, and he has decreed that the whole of the Military Secretariat of the War Cabinet from me downwards should be immediately suspended from duty while the culprits are discovered and suitably chastised.' He was laughing cheerfully and I felt a surge of true admiration for the sense and balance of this man. He knew just when things were really serious and just when they were exasperatingly silly. 'I am glad,' he went on, 'that you are taking your suspension in the right spirit,' and with that we parted happily.

It is a short step from him to the three men with whom he sat daily and nightly—the three Chiefs of Staff. My close observation of these three great figures dates from 1943 onwards—that is to say, from the days of Sir Alan Brooke, Sir Charles Portal and Sir Andrew Cunningham, as they then were. At that time Brooke and Portal were comparatively unknown to the public—far less well known than the Commanders, to whom in fact they gave orders and occasional rockets: Wavell, Tedder, Alexander, Bomber Harris, Montgomery, Wilson, Auchinleck, etc. It is true that Brooke had commanded a corps in France before Dunkirk and Portal had been Commander-in-Chief Bomber Command at the start of the war, but their operational fame, never great or widespread, was now forgotten, and the public had no idea of the responsibilities these men carried and the courage and singleness of purpose with which they discharged them. Cunningham had been a bold and daring Commander-in-Chief in the Mediterranean. His name was widely known and his repute was high.

Some thought that his gifts of command would be wasted in the high office of First Sea Lord—but it was not so. All three names are much more widely known now than they were then. At the end of the war the highest honours in the land were showered upon them. Since then Cunningham and Brooke have made themselves known by their books to a wider public; Portal characteristically has kept silence.

For about the last year of the war I saw these three men in daily conference together with General Ismay and attended and most faithfully and effectively served by a secretariat, in which the names of General Hollis, General Ian Jacob and Colonel C. R. Price are constant and prominent. As a result of war memoirs, individual histories (like Churchill's) and official histories, it is widely known that the fabrication of our victorious strategy was no easy process, that it was not only the complexity of the issues and the paucity of our resources which caused these difficulties, but also the clash and conflict of forceful personalities. Sir Winston's own record of the war leaves the reader in no doubt of his critical attitude to the Chiefs of Staff. He has printed some of the innumerable minutes with which he stimulated and provoked them. Until Lord Alanbrooke's diaries appeared it was uncertain how these minutes were received. Were they taken lying down? Was there immediate obedience? For Sir Winston has been careful to print none of the replies. Lord Alanbrooke's two volumes make abundantly clear how violent the reactions often were. Time and the measured judgments of historians will get the true balance long after we are dead.

For my part I was deeply impressed by the harmony prevailing between the three Chiefs of Staff. It is true, of course, that when the Prime Minister attacked them they closed their ranks. That was a cardinal point of their conduct. In the face of the Prime Minister their loyalty to each other must be invincible and impenetrable. There must be no defeating in detail. But, quite apart from the Prime Minister, there were many areas where the needs and aims of the three Services clashed, always a big margin for quarrelling, but the three Chiefs faced these difficulties squarely and never allowed them to delay or damage the prosecution of the war. The speed and efficiency with which the seemingly insoluble and intractable mass of daily business was despatched ought to be recorded to the eternal credit of the three Chiefs themselves, their own staffs in their own Services, the Joint Planning Staff, the inter-Service staff which served them in the War Cabinet Office, General Ismay and the Chiefs of Staff Secretariat.

It seemed to me, watching them daily with critical admiration from my level, that their personalities were largely complementary—the alert violence and speed of Brooke's thoughts and words, a touch of bravado from Cunningham, and the lucid calm intellectual strength of Portal, making in unity a formidable enemy for the German and Japanese High Commands and, it must be admitted, a rather formidable ally for the American Chiefs of Staff. Brooke was the Chairman and I should say the acknowledged leader. For the actual conduct of business I daresay Portal in the Chair would have done a tidier and more business-like job, but this side of the Chairman's task in fact mattered little with men like Hollis, Jacob and Price to pick up the bits. Brooke was the spokesman whether it was in Cabinet, with the Prime Minister, with visiting Ministers or Commanders, or with the United States Chiefs of Staff. On those who had never seen him before—or, for that matter, on those who saw him daily—he made an astonishing impact. A heavy, square man, with long arms, dark, aquiline features, strong, neat, well-groomed, trim dark moustache, a somewhat smouldering and disdainful air, his general appearance the traditional one of a handsome, smart and self-respecting soldier, but more powerful, more formidable. It was when he began to speak that the impact was felt in full. The voice was of the

metallic type, not disagreeably so, but no deep, rich or mellow
tones. What was so surprising, so unlooked for from that dark,
strong, somewhat brooding face, was the speed with which the
words issued forth, as rapid as machine-gun fire, a prolonged
burst and then a breath fetched hastily with a sort of indrawn
groan and then another unchecked burst. The boldest might
quail before this onslaught and many did. Even the French,
who came hoping to gain time for defence while the interpreters were at work, were disappointed; for Brooke was as
rapid in French as he was in English. It was frightening, this
direct assault, and it was sometimes incomprehensible. The
words tumbled over each other and any words that came to
hand were fired off indiscriminately. Germans became Russians,
Americans became Japanese, Rome found itself in Egypt and
Cairo on the Persian Gulf, Montgomery was defending Stalin-
grad and Stalin sitting in the White House. The combinations
were confusing and they became even worse if a report or
telegram had to be read out aloud by the C.I.G.S. Whole lines
were omitted and it required a lot of imagination to supply the
gaps. But there was never any question of taking advantage of
these strange slips of memory or quirks of interpretation. If you
had dared to interrupt with a demure and smug 'Sir, do you
mean Germans—or do you mean Alamein?' you would have
been blasted out of the room. It was perfectly clear what he
meant and if he chose to use different names and terms what
was that to us? He was right, he was the great man, stimulated,
inspired, dynamic. He had his faults, no doubt, but for the
prosecution of the war, for the management and control of its
higher direction, he was indispensable and he deserved all the
help and support that any of us could give him. He was not a
gracious or a graceful man, but he had an infectious sense of
humour and if that was tickled there came gusts and tears of
laughter which held me without question in the captivated
circle of his admirers. He once spat out at me a remark of

warm, personal congratulation, and even though he soon forgot me and my face those words remain in my memory to support and encourage me.

On his right at that daily meeting in a conference room in the Cabinet Office sat Admiral Sir Andrew Cunningham—somewhat irascible sea-dog, red-faced, squat and square. It always seemed as if anger and impatience were very near the surface. There was danger in the drooping bloodshot eye, and yet though sometimes short and sharp (as I have previously described) he was never wilfully obstructive or ill-tempered. In most of the matters under discussion he had less stake than the others and he is one of those admirable committee members who never say anything if there is nothing to say. When naval matters were under discussion he was crisp and to the point, very practical, of course, and not very willing to listen to what sometimes seemed to him the ill-informed opinions of land-lubbers. Though he was much more silent than the other two on the many politico-strategic problems, it would be wrong to think that he was ineffective. At unexpected moments and on unlikely topics I have known him suddenly produce timely and statesmanlike opinions. If, for example, as could happen, there was a note of contempt in the attitude of Brooke and Portal towards the requirements and aims of the lesser allies, Cunningham was quick to espouse their cause and to force the committee to take a more balanced and fair-minded view. This latent virtue in him was particularly valuable during the long arguments and discussions which preceded the meetings of the combined Chiefs of Staff—i.e. the British and American Chiefs of Staff sitting together. It is a matter of history that there were a good many strategic problems on which we did not see eye to eye with the Americans and in preparing for the discussion of these Brooke and Portal were busy adopting embattled positions and practising their tactics, working up arguments, anticipating the views of General Marshall and the others, deriding the conciliatory powers of Admiral Leahy, attributing ideas and policies which in all likelihood they would never advance. Cunningham would listen with diminishing patience to these increasingly far-fetched polemics and at last would intervene with saner and calmer counsels, bringing Brooke and Portal back to an amused surprise at themselves.

On the left of the First Sea Lord sat, by invitation, the Chief of Combined Operations. During the time of which I am writing Major-General Robert Laycock filled this position. The great majority of the topics considered by the Chiefs of Staff were no concern of his and during the discussion of these he kept a wise and modest silence. This unassuming, unobtrusive demeanour made his interventions into arguments about amphibious operations all the more effective. In these arguments his opinions were of the utmost importance. Indeed they might almost be called decisive, since it is perfectly true that for a large part of the war our strategy was hamstrung by the shortage of landing ships and craft. I think the three big Chiefs liked this exceptionally brave and modest man. He played his limited part with good sense and great charm and when his views encountered, as they often did, hot contempt and opposition from the First Sea Lord he took it all with grace and good humour.

On the left of the C.I.G.S. sat Marshal of the Royal Air Force Sir Charles Portal, the Chief of the Air Staff, in some respects the most remarkable of the three. He looked more like a medieval monk than a great commander—long and lean and pale, narrow head, receding hair, deep furrows in his cheeks, and an immense, strong, dominating nose. His war-time leanness suited him and it might almost have been said of him that in those days he had reached the point where ugliness is indistinguishable from beauty. He was a devoted and dedicated man. Nothing must interfere with the exact and continuous performance of his duty—not fun, nor friendship, nor laughter, no diversions whatever except a very occasional day's fishing. He ordered his private life to accord with this inexorable regimen. He lived, I think, in the Dorchester Hotel, not to enjoy its luxury, but to escape the press of domestic problems and the social attentions of relations and friends. He took his meals quite frequently in the Travellers' Club, hurrying in blinkers straight to the dining-room and straight out again, sitting throughout his frugal meal with a book open on the table and his eyes never moving beyond his plate and the pages of his book. His power of concentration was intense, his ability to work very long hours of deep intellectual effort un-matched. This manner of life was deliberate, not spontaneous. I have never known him well, but he is by no means the frigid recluse that he appeared to be in those war years. His country needed all his nervous energy. There was none to spare for the normal trivialities of human intercourse. It was said of him that he was cold-blooded, inhuman. It was reported to him that some of his own staff in the Air Ministry, brilliant hand-picked officers, were overworking to the point of breakdown. Would he not give them some leave or send them to open-air duties for a time? It is said that he peremptorily refused to consider any such thing. Officers were being killed on operations; why should they not be killed doing their duty in Whitehall? I have no idea whether he really said this, but, even if he did, he was demanding no more of them than he demanded of himself. Years later he told me that Winston had included in his book a minute to him earnestly requesting that he should take more care of himself and work less hard. He had never seen any such minute, he assured me with much amusement. I suggested that Winston probably had sent it, but that C.A.S.'s own staff, knowing his views on work in war-time, had been afraid to show it to him. He did not demur.

The habitual self-denial and self-discipline brought their reward. His mind and understanding were absolutely clear, his

grasp of any problem immediate and exact, his reasoning lucid
and objective, his conclusions definite and clearly expressed,
his manner unruffled, patient, but not without a touch of
contempt if he thought he was dealing with dense or inferior
minds. He was much more than the master of air strategy and
the commander of his own Service. He, like Brooke, saw the
much wider implications and, less impetuously than Brooke,
weighed them up with measured care and discrimination. At
times the problems which faced these three men were of such
complexity, calling for the consideration of all kinds of military
and non-military factors, that it was a matter of extreme
intellectual difficulty to present in comprehensible written form
the arguments on which their final decision was based. But this
had to be done, whether as a justification to the Prime Minister,
or as a reasoned explanation to different Commanders-in-Chief.
General Ismay and his staff were extremely adept at this kind of
thing, but once or twice I have seen even General Ismay quail
at the task. On such occasions Portal would come to the rescue.
'It is quite easy,' he would say, without much tact, and then
give out in lucid order the factors and conclusions of a perfect
minute. I found a great deal to admire and to emulate in this
remote and impersonal man, but it came as a surprise to me to
find out that he was not in fact remote or impersonal. Just before
I was demobilised he stopped me one day in the passage, knew
my name, knew about me, praised my work, enquired about
my future plans, all with charm and humour. The war was over
and he felt able to give rein to his natural friendliness once more.

Once a week the Directors of Plans themselves attended the
meeting of the Chiefs of Staff and on these occasions the
secretariat put on the Agenda two or three reports by the Joint
Planning Staff so that the Directors could defend their views in
person to the Chiefs of Staff. On one of these occasions Antony
Head, who was then a Brigadier at Combined Operations
Headquarters and represented them at meetings of the Joint

Planning Staff, and I devised a form of cricket. The Directors of
Plans were the batsmen and the three Chiefs of Staff were the
bowlers, while Antony and I surreptitiously kept the bowling
analysis. I have lost the actual document on which in approved
form we had recorded the overs bowled by each Chief, but the
result I remember very well, and nothing I think could give a
fairer idea of the particular powers and virtue of each. Cunningham bowled very little. With Brooke he shared the new ball
and he made it swing alarmingly in the air, but he was more
ferocious than accurate and so long as the batsmen retained
their nerve he could generally be mastered and hit hard to the
boundary. He bowled, I think, only about four overs, he took
one wicket with a fast inswinging yorker and ended up with an
analysis of about one for twenty. Brooke at the other end
bowled extremely fast. He should have been no-balled several
times for asking incomprehensible questions such as 'Why do
you say the Germans will hang on to Rangoon?' but nobody
dared do this and it made him all the harder to play. He wanted
very careful watching. Much of it was a bit short of a length
and came up awkwardly, but there was an occasional loose one
which the Directors thankfully despatched for four. His
analysis came out at about three for forty-eight. Portal was slow
and steady, immaculate length, never a bad ball. Maiden
followed maiden and sometimes he got one to turn nastily and
it was by no means easy to detect the googly. In a long-sustained spell of intelligent bowling he took four for thirty-seven.
Throughout this performance Head and I felt like two idle
schoolboys—and that is what we were. I have often wondered
what would have happened if the C.I.G.S. had seen us and said,
'What are you doing there under the table?' I almost wish he
had. The ensuing rocket would have been one to treasure.

   Apart from the regular weekly attendance of the Directors
of Plans other persons from time to time attended meetings of
the Chiefs of Staff for the discussion of particular items. There

were Commanders-in-Chief who had been called home for consultation, Ministers who wanted to impress upon the Chiefs of Staff the importance of some particular factor which was their concern, representatives of Allied Governments, of General de Gaulle and of the United States Chiefs of Staff in London, and during the preparation of Overlord General Morgan, known as Cossac, and subsequently General Eisenhower, the Supreme Commander, and his Chief of Staff, General Bedell Smith. In this way I had glimpses of other prominent men of the time. I remember Herbert Morrison discussing V.2s with the Chiefs of Staff, making little headway in his approach to this powerful body. I remember Lord Leathers, a fairly frequent visitor to Chiefs of Staff meetings. No operations of any kind were possible without ships and Lord Leathers and his Ministry had to be consulted and cajoled at all levels. One long argument between him and the Chiefs of Staff I remember vividly, Lord Leathers obstructing and objecting for all his worth and emphasising his points with a corkscrew motion of his hand and arm pointed at the midriff of the C.I.G.S., whose rapid rage mounted alarmingly. When at last the argument ceased, and Lord Leathers left the room, Brooke immediately imitated this strange corkscrew gesture, shouting out at the same time, 'I hope he is not a twister like that!'

Of General Eisenhower my recollection is faint. One day we travelled up in our antiquated lift together—he and I and General Bedell Smith, his Chief of Staff. He was complimentary, he knew the great work done by the Joint Planning Staff, the help it was giving to him as Supreme Commander for Overlord. Together we went into the meeting place of the Chiefs of Staff. He was impressive in a certain sense, but not as impressive as I had hoped and expected. He was determined, it was clear, to keep his mind free from detail and to grapple with major issues only. This was never exactly the mood of Brooke or Portal. They did not believe that the major issues could be clear to them until they themselves had fought their way through the dense jungle of detail. I felt, I must confess, some slight twinge of shame at seeing the Supreme Commander so often floored by Brooke's battery of comment and taking refuge in 'Oh! that is a matter of detail. Perhaps we could leave that to my Chief of Staff.' I was conscious of the unexpressed disdain of Brooke and Portal. And yet I daresay General Eisenhower was right. He knew his own capacity and he knew, perhaps more clearly than anyone, the complex political problems which were to confront him every day. He had, after all, already lived through the Darlan episode and I have no doubt he was expecting worse to come. He was going to need all his nervous energy for dealing with the sullen pride of General de Gaulle and the impertinence and insubordination of one of his Army Group Commanders. A more practised and experienced military mind would probably have judged differently the strategy of the advance into Germany, but I do not feel sure that what is now generally regarded as the incorrect strategy which the Supreme Commander adopted was due to military incompetence or inexperience. If General Alexander had been commanding 21 Army Group the British view would probably have prevailed.

It was at one of these meetings that I first saw General Slim. He was reporting to the Chiefs of Staff the situation in Burma and doing it, I thought, very effectively, with firmness and precision and a welcome economy of words. The strong chin, the rugged masculine air, impressed me, but not more than the persistent twinkle of humour in his eyes. I came to know this man better when he was C.I.G.S. and again when he was Governor-General of Australia and I was British High Commissioner in New Zealand. The more I knew him, the more my admiration increased. With every job he did his stature grew. He is a full man with a rich personality, direct, fearless, humorous, sensitive, missing nothing, pretending nothing, one of the most complete, best-balanced, most significant men I have known. Not very long ago I happened to sit behind him at the Royal Court Theatre on the opening night of Ionesco's *Exit the King*. This play runs for ninety difficult minutes of intellectual concentration without rest or intermission of any kind. At the—to me merciful—end of the performance Slim turned round to tell me that on the whole he approved. He had then only recently returned from being Governor-General in Australia and I reflected on the disciplined and courteous patience which vice-regal duties impose upon a man. Real kings can be less circumspect and I remembered how it was recorded of King George V that after three or four hours of boredom he had remarked sharply that he would sooner abdicate than witness another performance of *Hamlet*.

H

3

War-time Conferences

THREE times I was included in the staff which attended the full-scale meetings of President and Prime Minister and British and American Chiefs of Staff. I was at Cairo in November 1943, at the second Quebec Conference in September 1944 and at Potsdam in July 1945. These were great occasions and I do not think any sensitive man could have taken part in them without the feeling that men were seeking to control their destiny and that history was being made. When I was told that I was to go to Cairo my pride and excitement were intense and I longed to tell my family and my friends of my good fortune, and to share with them my thrill of adventure. But, of course, I had to keep my mouth shut. The time and place of these Conferences were deadly secrets. A well-placed torpedo or a bomb or two could have wiped out all the Allied leaders at one stroke. I had to explain my month's absence by some plausible cover plan, and indeed it had become by then a habit of mind to tell nobody anything, in company to play the village idiot, to stare uncomprehendingly at awkward questioners, to make no comment by word or gesture on the wild speculations and rumours that filled the air. We must have seemed dull dogs indeed and no doubt many people wondered why officers with such dim and unenquiring minds were put into such important positions. But it was the only safe way. Our minds were so stocked with military information that I, at any rate, could never have been sure about any one item of it whether I had read it in a newspaper or a top-secret telegram.

Cairo

Secrecy surrounded us from the start, though I doubt if all the security arrangements were well conceived. For example, our departure by train from London took place from Addison Road Station. There assembled on a platform hardly ever used at any other time were the three Chiefs of Staff and all their staffs and a good many other high-ranking officers who had come to see them off. The citizens of Kensington and Hammersmith can hardly have failed to notice this unlooked-for galaxy as they passed upon their way and to have concluded, 'Another of those Conferences, I suppose!' When we went to Cairo we sailed from Plymouth in H.M.S. *Renown* and on the very next night Plymouth was subjected to an air raid. I do not know if this was a leakage of information or a coincidence. Doubts about security haunted the opening of this Conference, although I did not realize it at the time. It was feared that the Germans knew that we were all bound for Cairo, and, as Cairo was within easy striking distance of German airfields in Crete, frantic last-minute efforts were made to change the venue. Malta had only recently been freed from its long ordeal of siege and bombardment and the thought of holding the Conference in its bent and battered palaces appealed to some romantic

minds. A hasty survey was made, but the project was proved to
be totally impracticable. At length it was decided to stick to the
original plan and accept what risk there was. In fact nothing
untoward occurred, nothing to test the marksmanship of the
A.A. gunners installed in the vicinity of the Mena House Hotel.

I myself was unaware of these hesitations and changes of
plan. With a number of other staff officers and W.R.N.S.
officers I transhipped at Algiers into the cruiser *London* and we
proceeded rapidly on our way to Alexandria. There were still
German submarines in the Mediterranean and German aircraft
based in Greece and Crete. If you were making an unescorted
journey it was as well to hurry—and we did. Upon going on
board I was surprised and flattered to find that I, an unimportant Lieutenant-Colonel, had been allotted the Admiral's day
cabin. This seemed to me kindness and courtesy beyond anything I could reasonably expect. The cabin itself was comparatively spacious and well equipped and so long as we remained
in Algiers harbour I was pleased to the point of smugness. As
soon as we left harbour and set off in the open sea I realised that
I was not as lucky as I had imagined. The cabin was as far aft as
it could be, immediately above the screws, and once we had
attained twenty-five knots, at which we remained for the rest
of the journey, the whole cabin shook and rattled with the
violence of a devil's kitchen. It was quite impossible to lay one's
head upon the pillow. It was at once banged and bashed violently up and down and sideways like a fives ball in an Eton
fives court. To avoid a permanent confusion of wits I spent the
nights in a chair and borrowed Dick Craddock's cabin, which
was amidships, to get some sleep in the afternoons. Apart from
this unusual but unimportant discomfort, this rapid voyage in
a very happy ship stands out in my memory as one of the most
cheerful periods in the war—much laughter, much gaiety and
much fun.

On arrival at Alexandria we were at once ordered to stay on

board, out of sight. No reasons were given. Within a few hours we were ordered to disembark, but before we could do so we were once again ordered to stay where we were. This series of order and counter-order, though we had no idea of it then, was dictated by the security fear to which I have referred before. To us it merely seemed an irritating muddle, marked in my memory chiefly by an accident to Jimmy Green, my chief clerk. He was standing on the jetty with his back to the ship discussing with others the difficult job of unloading and shifting all our secret documents. Without thinking he took a step back and fell between jetty and ship's side into the filthy oily water of Alexandria harbour. Fortunately he was speedily and safely pulled out, but he had to spend a long time and much toil in getting his hair and his skin free of oil. At last we were told to disembark and get ourselves into waiting motor-cars which drove us off without further delays to the Mena House Hotel, the whole of which had been requisitioned for the Conference. Hastily we set up our offices, disposed our secret documents, got ourselves into posture for three weeks of planning, arguing and maintaining, re-planning, drafting and re-drafting, long, wearisome, urgent hours of it, getting our own minds clear, making sure of our facts and the soundness of our assumptions, persuading, cajoling our American colleagues, insisting that our judgments were more experienced, our convictions more realistic. It must have tried their patience and good humour to be told so often—or at least for gentle hints to be dropped here and there—that we had been in the war a good deal longer than they had. This weapon should have been used sparingly. It could be a boomerang; for it was only in the last year that we had made much of a job of it. But we all got along pretty well in spite of deep differences of approach and expression. At our level American officers were allowed almost no discretion, no flexibility, no deviation from some hideous form of words, cacophonous to our ears and largely meaningless, stilted,

stereotyped jargon, designed, it seemed, to defeat action, to tie
down those smart British in fetters of verbiage. For a whole
night I wrestled with them, the last night of the Conference, to
produce a joint paper which had some life and meaning. I was
nimbler than they. I ran round them and wore them down,
retiring now and again to my corner for slugs of orange juice,
and when the dawn came their bleared eyes were grateful for
the sight of a completed paper to submit to the combined
Chiefs of Staff. They signed it without further fight and with
characteristic American generosity and good nature they
remembered this night when recommending me for a Legion
of Merit.

To me, to all of us, I suppose, this Conference at Cairo was
a very strange interlude. The great war leaders, the President of
the U.S.A., the Prime Minister of Great Britain, the General-
issimo and Madame Chiang Kai-shek, and all the mighty
Chiefs of Staff and great Commanders meeting in this ancient
city, as once again the Pyramids looked down upon the
making of history. I had never been in Cairo before and in
those few weeks several things became very clear to me—first
and foremost the deep-seated hatred of the Egyptians for the
British. We had occupied and overrun their capital city. We
had to, of course; it was war and we could not for our own
strategic reasons let Egypt fall to Italians and Germans. It would
have been blatant hypocrisy to pretend that we had defended
Egypt out of love for King Farouk and his people. We did not
so pretend. I do not think we bothered to ask the King's
permission to hold our Conference in his capital. If we did he
had no option but to agree. Cairo was full of British soldiers,
the staffs of G.H.Q. Middle East, always in Churchill's estima-
tion grossly inflated, soldiers on leave, drafts arriving. Shep-
heard's Hotel was a gay meeting place for the British and their
friends, night clubs were run for the British, the Gezira Club
was a British country club. There were, of course, some rich

Egyptians who liked all this, who profited from it, finding their own pockets more important than their country's dignity. I could not help feeling that the country was decadent and demoralised, debauched and despised by the occupying Power, divided between attitudes of impotent hostility and cringing subservience, a disunited feudal society. In the bedrooms at the Mena House Hotel instructions for the use of the bell were thus expressed—'One ring for the waiter, two for the chambermaid and three for the native'; and when you rang three times a miserable cringing creature appeared, to clean your shoes or empty your slops; and officers who had been in Egypt before treated this poor degraded specimen of humanity with callous contempt. In a brief interlude I visited the Sphinx in company with a certain Major-General who thought it good form and good fashion to treat the guide with facetious insolence, spoiling for me the deep inscrutable significance of this most impressive relic of antiquity. The streets of Cairo were squalid, almost every house infested with bugs and fleas, the people dirty and bedraggled. The beauty and luxuriance of the Delta, the colours of the bougainvillaea and hibiscus, the velvety softness of the night sky and the silent mustering of the rich and golden dawn were in lovely contrast with the mean arrogance of Man and his works.

Here for the first time I saw the U.S. Chiefs of Staff sitting with the British Chiefs of Staff as the combined Chiefs of Staff Committee. I was impressed by what seemed to me the broad statesmanlike approach of General Marshall, somewhat awed by the cold, critical and extremely laconic comments of Admiral King, widely reported to be violently anti-British, without doubt more interested in the Pacific war, and surprised by the slow flat drawl of Admiral Leahy who presided without managing to give any direction or life to the proceedings. At this stage of the war I could not feel very much harmony or unity of purpose at this level and it was hard bargaining and hard argument all the way. The cream of the Conference, the Prime Minister and President, the Chiefs of Staff and a very few senior staff officers, went off in the middle of the proceedings to Teheran for the first official conference with our curiously hostile and graceless Russian ally. We remained in Cairo in comparative tranquillity but much occupied in preparing for the return of the great. The heat was still considerable, the mosquitoes numerous, the food too rich, and perhaps too carelessly prepared, for our pinched war-time digestions. I succumbed for a day or two to a recurrence of phlebitis in my leg and I remember lying on my bed discussing with General Whiteley the directive for the Supreme Commander in Algiers and then in imperial grandeur dictating a draft from my supine position.

The great returned, the concluding problems were hammered out, the final reports prepared, my long night of conflict with the American planners was played out, there was a session of doubt and perplexity with General Ismay, who suddenly seemed finished, breathless, almost inanimate—and we dispersed. I travelled to Alexandria and rejoined H.M.S. *London*, with some, but not all, of my previous companions. We were, perhaps, a little deflated—long struggles, intense argument, deep concentration—and at the end an elaborate and effective papering over of the cracks and not much conviction of harmony and constructive decision—and yet enough to make the war go on towards our ultimate victory.

The journey home in H.M.S. *London* remains in my memory for various reasons. The uncomplaining resignation with which I had accepted the skull-bashing of the Admiral's cabin on the way out earned me a comfortable cabin amidships on the way back, and, what was more, the ready friendship of the ship's officers. Again we battered our way along at twenty-five knots. As we passed within range of German aircraft in Crete there was an alarm and we anxiously occupied our appointed action stations, which turned out to be, as far as we passengers were concerned, stations of complete and useless inaction. Nothing happened and we belted on, passing close to Pantellaria, which the Prime Minister had once described as a priceless strategic rock, vainly insisting upon its capture. With difficulty he accepted the advice of the Chiefs of Staff that its strategic value was negligible and that the resources required for its capture were quite out of proportion to any advantage we might gain.

In safety we reached the calm of Gibraltar harbour, expecting a brief respite only, but there was an unexpected delay of two or three days for what reason we did not at first discern. I used these days to explore the rock and to wonder at the blue and golden view across the Straits. I visited some coast-defence gunners who were manning the 9 ft 2 in. guns mounted on the top of the rock to give us command of the Straits. Up to that point of time, December 1943, they had never been fired and I think they never were. The poor gunners, some of whom had been there all the war, felt very much neglected and very much out of the war, forgotten, useless. We spent a cheerful evening together and they begged me on return to London to try to get them a reprieve. I never heard what happened. At last we learned the cause of our delay. The Prime Minister, who was to have joined us in Gibraltar and returned home in *King George V*, was ill in Carthage and likely to be so for some time. We were to wait no longer and with foreboding in our hearts we left the calm waters of the Straits and beat out many miles into the Atlantic, to escape the attention of German aircraft, before turning north. Here we encountered a full Atlantic gale and very rough seas, which forced us to reduce speed. I shall not forget the almost tragic sight of the mighty battleship *King George V* ahead of us wallowing miserably in these tremendous troughs. She looked a good deal more uncomfortable than we felt in our much smaller ship.

The Second Quebec

That was the first of these exciting interludes, not to be repeated for nearly a year, and before we set out again Overlord had taken place, we were firmly established in France, Paris had been liberated and the abominable V.1s and V.2s had begun to rain down upon us. The end of the war with Germany was in sight, but there were still many problems to be settled and many plans to be made for the defeat of Japan. Contention on these matters was fierce and continuous, not only between us and the Americans, but between the British Chiefs of Staff and the Prime Minister. Once again we assembled in our glory at Addison Road Station and this time our special train took us to the Clyde where we embarked in *Queen Mary*. This great ship, which travelled unescorted at great speeds from one side of the Atlantic to the other, which with the *Queen Elizabeth* was one of the biggest factors in making Overlord possible, had been specially fitted up and adjusted for this memorable return trip. The ship was a troopship, carrying at peak periods as many as 16,000 troops, who took their meals twice a day in shifts and in summer weather slept on deck in shifts too. For this trip a portion of the ship had been smartened up and segregated for the Prime Minister and his considerable entourage of Service and civilian advisers and helpers. We were comfortable and well cared for, well fed, and there was a bar especially rigged up and stocked for our stimulation. We needed it. As we zigzagged our way at twenty-eight or thirty knots through the torrid temperatures of the Gulf Stream the Chiefs of Staff found themselves locked in combat with the Prime Minister, striving against his ill-health and tiresome temperament to reach an agreed strategy before we met the Americans in Quebec. We had a great deal of work, reports to the Chiefs of Staff, draft minutes by the Chiefs of Staff to the Prime Minister, and I found myself hot and harassed and busy. In the morning I would attend a meeting of the Chiefs of Staff in a stateroom to listen to their deliberations and opinions, to get from them a rough idea of the arguments and proposals they would like to put forward to the Prime Minister. The deliberations were not always easy to follow. There were unexpected distractions in this stateroom in the *Queen Mary*. When it seemed that agreement between the Chiefs of Staff was near, when Portal or Ismay had begun a summary of the main points on which the Joint Planning Staff might get to work, there would be a sudden hitch, a hesitation, because the attention of the C.I.G.S. had been deflected and he was busy drawing the ducks in flight which adorned the polished wooden panels of the cabin. In the afternoon and evening I wrestled with the Planners to produce the reports and draft minutes which the Chiefs of Staff needed —long talk and argument with an occasional visit from Ismay to help us with suggestions and ideas. It was a warm and busy time, but it had its moments of fun and laughter, more particularly because I had brought with me as my chief helper Wing Commander Alan Houseman, from that day until his untimely death one of my closest friends and advisers. He knew when and how to distract me from the straits of frigid duty and how to give genuine and valuable assistance in the daily struggle by taking off me some of the dull routine and by offering extremely bright suggestions when all seemed black and sombre.

On arrival at Halifax we embarked in a special train which took us the long haul to Quebec. I remember nothing of this long railway journey except that at some station, where we stopped and stretched our legs, I paid a visit to the vast engine and mounted the cab for a chat with the engine-driver. As I tinkered with the knobs and handles he suggested pulling one which I took to be the whistle. In innocence I pulled and the effect was to blow volumes of soot out of the funnel to cover my friends and colleagues who were walking peacefully about the platform. I remained secreted in the cab until they had all hastened back into the train, blackened and irritated.

At Quebec the whole of the Château Frontenac Hotel had been commandeered to house the Conference and all the participants. After blacked-out, pinched and wretched London it was luxury itself. Everything was beautifully organised—thanks largely to Joan Bright and her helpers—the food was excellent and there was an air of gaiety, even a small night club, to disperse the strains and struggles of the day at about 11 p.m. As usual there was not much spare time, but enough for some quick shopping in Quebec and for a visit to the Heights of Abraham to relive the drama of Wolfe and Montcalm. On the last day Alan Houseman organised a day by a lake in the country for the members of the Joint Planning Staff—fishing, bathing and excellent picnic—and it was I think the first and only fine day. On the last day but one I happened to be lunching at the same table as Joan Bright and I ventured to regret that we had not had better weather. She had suffered much throughout the Conference from frivolous and tiresome complaints from officers and others who ought to have been on their knees in gratitude, and in consequence her nerves were somewhat strained. Upon hearing yet another complaint—very mildly critical of the clerk of the weather and not of her—her nerves snapped and she let fly. I ought to be ashamed of myself, after all the comfort and luxury showered upon me free of charge and all the work done for me by these hospitable Canadians, to make snivelling complaints about a drop of rain. My extreme surprise and startled looks at this unexpected blitzkrieg soon turned the attack to laughter, which to this day we often recall.

The internal dissension, the uneasy rub between the Chiefs of Staff and the Prime Minister, which preceded this Conference and which continued unabated till we reached Halifax, had led us to expect a more than usually difficult task in agreeing with the Americans a strategy for the overthrow of Germany and the prosecution of the war against Japan, which would also receive the assent of President and Prime Minister. But all went much more easily than we had expected and agreements for the British share in operations against Japan, even for the participation of the Royal Navy in the Pacific Fleet, encountered much less opposition than students of Admiral King's intentions and attitudes had dared to prophesy. Looking back on it now I cannot remember any grave difficulties at the level of the Combined Staff Planners at this Conference. Some arguments and misunderstandings occurred, of course, but the combined planning by British and American staffs was very much easier and very much more effective than it had been at Cairo. At all levels, as usual, there were difficulties about shipping and certainly the rapid shift of shipping resources from Europe to the Far East was bound to be desperately complex. I remember well General Holmes, then Director of Movements at the War Office, being sent for one morning by the British Chiefs of Staff and instructed to write a paper on some aspect of this problem for consideration the following day, before the Chiefs of Staff were due to defend their position against the Americans in the Combined Chiefs of Staff. The paper was duly written and circulated in time for the meeting of the British Chiefs of Staff next morning. When the Chiefs of Staff reached this item on their Agenda the C.I.G.S. started to deliver a violent attack upon the paper, seemingly addressing his remarks to me sitting opposite to him at the far end of the table. Before he had got very far in his tirade Ismay suggested that General Holmes had better be brought into the meeting to explain the paper. Thankfully I dashed out of the room to find him; and there he was quite close to the door, smiling away to himself and hoping no doubt for this very opportunity to exhibit in person his grasp of the problem. There was no time to warn him as I bustled him into the room. With the air of a man about to receive a congratulatory address he complacently took his seat beside the First Sea Lord and turned expectantly to face the C.I.G.S. There followed a withering blast. I never saw a man's expression and demeanour change so quickly and so decisively; in the twinkling of an eye poor General Holmes became a frightened schoolboy, trying in vain to excuse himself, or a beaten boxer hopelessly attempting to ward off the unintermitted rain of blows. Every attempted explanation was brushed roughly aside before it had got under way. Any question was shouted down. General Holmes had to make what he could of it and like a beaten dog he crept from the room to try once more. I forget the sequel but I expect we all put our heads together and agreed upon an interpretation of the C.I.G.S.'s angry and incomprehensible verbosity and General Holmes quickly produced an acceptable paper.

These things had to be done at speed. There was no sitting back and taking your time at these Conferences. There was a limited number of days in which decisions had to be taken and the arguments and discussions which led to these decisions were continuous and intensive. It was no good claiming that two days' delay for reflection would probably give birth to a wiser conclusion. In two days the Conference would be over and all the chief decision-takers dispersed to the four corners of the earth. If no conclusion was reached by 11 p.m. then the discussion must be continued until a conclusion was reached. It was always tough going, but it was tough going of a different kind. In London work was just as heavy and continuous and the answer was often required the next morning. But sometimes it was not. Sometimes there could be two days for further reflection. And in London there was very little to do except work. There were no doubt night clubs and late-night amusements, but we had long since forgotten about these. So far as I was concerned there were one or two private houses—notably

Nancy Frazer's flat in Grosvenor Street—where you could be sure of warm hospitality, pleasant company, lively conversation and as much as you wanted to drink, but apart from occasional visits to these, our chief relaxation was local jokes and supper in the mess or a quick dinner at the club and work again thereafter. At these Conferences we tried to make up for our rather joyless existence in London. It was fun to get to that night club in the Château Frontenac for an hour or two before bed. One could always make up sleep, one hoped, on the way home. It was fun, too, to enjoy good meals and plenty of illumination and to feel oneself safely out of range of the baleful attentions of the enemy. In consequence life at Quebec was intensely concentrated, a combination of long hours of strenuous work and brief hours of pleasure and of sleep.

It lasted all too short a time and very soon we were on our way back to London. This time we took the long train journey from Quebec to New York and there once again embarked in *Queen Mary*. This time the Chiefs of Staff were not with us and the Prime Minister was tired and needed rest after the strenuous days of argument and decision. He retired to his staterooms and was not often seen. We were able to relax, to roam about this great ship, to survey with quiet thoughts the vast expanses of the Atlantic, as I often did from the eyes of the ship—until some zealous bridge officer thought that the sight of a Lieutenant-Colonel standing on the very sharpest point, staring 'with a wild surmise', might give some notions and expectations to a German periscope, and ordered me away. It had seemed to me a harmless position and one from which 'I could shoot my being through earth, sea, and air'—but I had to accept the cautious discipline transmitted from the bridge. Inside the ship, divorced from air, sea and sky, confined in this vast and airless hotel, we were comfortable enough in segregated cabins and our own bar. Thousands of American soldiers inhabited the ship with us, for them a brief interlude between their homes in the Middle West or the deep South and the battlefields of Western Europe—a rather comfortless voyage for them, cramped quarters, two meals a day, each moment further from their homes and closer to battles and dangers. The residue of amenities in the ship included the cinema and I remember well watching a film about President Wilson—a man who had been to my youth the philosopher king, the idealist saviour of mankind. I recall little of the film, but I happened to be sitting almost exactly behind the Prime Minister, who was throughout interested and attentive; and what excited me most was his reaction to the scene in which Wilson dismisses with arrogant and dignified contumely the German Ambassador, (Count von Bernstorff,) upon the imminent outbreak of war between the U.S.A. and Germany. Wilson's anger and indignation were overpowering, penetrating—the kind of alarming fury which must be expected from a patient and liberal man whose trust has been outraged. It was a moving scene, made more moving and more memorable to me because I overhead the Prime Minister say to his neighbours: 'I think that is very near the truth. I believe he did talk to Bernstorff very much like that.'

Our rapid voyage across the Atlantic, so far as I knew, was uneventful. At about twenty-eight knots we zigzagged our way in safety through calm and friendly seas; but as we came in pressing haste into the Clyde our luck deserted us and a seaman engaged upon some urgent duty fell into the sea and, in spite of hurried attention and search, was not picked up—drowned instantly perhaps, or cruelly mangled by those mighty screws—name unknown to me but an uneasy ghost to trouble the joy of my safe return.

The months that followed were uneasy and frustrating. Expectations of an early end to the war against Germany were disappointed and it became clear that there would be no surrender before the early summer at the best. Nevertheless the end was clearly in sight. It was a matter of time only and a short time at that before the Hitler regime and the German Army were obliterated. Immediately there was an urgent need for many politico-strategic decisions about the control of a defeated Germany and her allies and satellites—decisions, moreover, in which the Russians had to be intimately involved. Once again the Conference wheels were set in motion, but this time the British and Americans were the guests of the Russians at Yalta in February 1944. I myself was not included in the staffs which attended this epoch-making Conference, from which uneasy and dangerous consequences flowed and still flow. I was left behind to mind the shop at home and my Guardian Angel protected me even from being included in a late reinforcement of staff officers which was flown out at short notice only to crash off Lampedusa with but one survivor. In this tragic mishap many of my friends and fellow workers, whose abilities could ill be spared, most untimely perished.

Potsdam

The final Conference of the war took place at Potsdam two months after Germany's defeat and I had the good fortune to be present as a member of General Ismay's staff, assisting General Hollis with the Chiefs of Staff Committee and, as usual, looking after the Joint Planning Staff, who were, of course, an essential part of the machinery of these Conferences. I was elated. Never in my most sanguine moments had I imagined that I would find myself proudly seated, among the great ones of the earth, in the capital city of our defeated foe,

I

helping, in my small corner, to dictate terms and conditions to an implacable and uncivilised enemy. In this mood of excited pride I embarked in an aeroplane on a very hot day to fly to Gatow Airport at Berlin. The plane was full of staff officers and officials, most of whom seemed content to drowse heavily through the hot afternoon. But Norman Brook and I, in a romantic and perhaps naive mood of exultation, were determined to miss nothing. To the irritation of our fellow passengers we peered and pushed about, intent on seeing all we could of the devastation of the Ruhr, the results of a vast expenditure of material resources and of human life and courage. From this day and from this community of mood I date my close friendship with Brook.

From Gatow we drove to our appointed enclave at Babelsberg, a smart and popular summer resort on the Wannsee hard by Potsdam. The whole area was, of course, in the occupation of the Russian Army and the several miles of road which separated Gatow from Babelsberg were lined by Russian soldiers, standing, it seemed, shoulder to shoulder, bucolic, inattentive, unsmart, but creating at once in my mind the impression of the limitless resources of Russian man-power. The traffic-control points seemed for the most part to be manned by women, strong, robust, Amazonian types, totally devoid of feminine charm. In Babelsberg 2nd Army had made arrangements for us. We were lodged in different villas and there was a central mess with garden down to the lake and various committee rooms and offices in other villas. Everything had had to be improvised at short notice and without much help from the insensitive occupying Power. The villas had been luxurious, the resorts of rich Germans with their mistresses, but now they were bare and uncared for after years of war. The weather was very hot and the mosquitoes against which there were no curtains of defence made sleep difficult. In the mess we fed well and comfortably, but complained bitterly about the cost of the Rhine wine. To what end, then, had we defeated these Germans? Some method was found of reducing the price and we enjoyed a taste denied to most of us for several years. Spare time in the evening was made charming and agreeable by the performances of the R.A.F. orchestra, under Denis Matthews.

So far as I was concerned there was plenty of work, since each day I danced attendance upon both the Chiefs of Staff Committee and the Joint Planning Staff, but if the military content of this Conference had been the normal load my dual role would have been impossible. It was not. Germany was prostrate and it was only the politico-strategic measures for her control that occupied our minds. Japan had yet to be defeated and, as the secret of the atom bomb was rightly undisclosed on our level, we took no account of it in our plans. Our main difficulty as usual was shipping. How could we redeploy our shipping resources fast enough to bring our full weight of power to bear against Japan at a very early date? How could we do this and at the same time improve, if possible, the scope and volume of the imports into the United Kingdom, so long working and existing on a shoe-string? These were very complex problems in which I became, without quite knowing how or why, heavily involved and somewhat pushed and battered first by the Joint Planners, then by the Chiefs of Staff, then by the egregious Lord Leathers and by Lord Cherwell, then back and forth between the British and United States Chiefs of Staff, a process of rough negotiation in which Lieutenant-General Sir Gordon MacCready, Commander of the British Army Staff in Washington, played the chief part with a wise and experienced cunning.

Plans for the defeat of Japan led us to a full-scale tripartite Chiefs of Staff meeting—British, U.S. and Russian Chiefs of Staff sitting together in full power and panoply. General Hollis took me with him to make the record. The meeting took place on a very hot afternoon in the Cecilienhof, once the Potsdam home of the late Crown Prince who had built it in the style of a Tudor manor house. We were kept waiting for ten minutes or more in what had been the Crown Prince's study, a comfortable conventional English upper-class study, lined with books. I cannot now remember what classes of books there were, though all, I think, were beautifully bound in calf or in some similar style. To suit such deliberately English surroundings, the books, I should guess, were for the most part about field sports. I took an inconspicuous seat and waited. The three Chiefs of Staff showed an active and excited interest in the contents of the shelves, and each one, finding some books, on fishing very likely, which took his fancy, handed them with glee to an A.D.C., presumably as the justifiable loot of the victor.

We moved into a large room for the meeting and took our places round a large table—twenty or more of us at the table with interpreters and some additional staff officers behind us. Admiral Leahy opened the proceedings, extending an elaborate and polysyllabic welcome to the Chiefs of Staff of what he called, by a drowsy slip of the tongue, 'Our gallant ally Japan'. It was growing very hot. It did not matter. The interpreters were not such fools and the Russians easily sustained their blank and uncomprehending stares. The proceedings took a dull, laborious turn. The U.S. Chiefs of Staff, each in turn, gave his appreciation of the strategic situation in the Japanese war—all dull and dry and turgid. The British followed, a little crisper perhaps, but we had heard it all before. The room grew hotter and, as the Russians began their appreciations, the struggle to fight off sleep became almost insupportable. The suspicion of a snore not far away brought me to my full senses, and there was General Ismay, an unconditional victim of Morpheus. General Hollis nudged me and smiled knowingly. In a few minutes he was out himself. Nothing could have galvanised me more successfully. Somebody had to remember what had been said and agreed and my two Generals were for the moment lost to oblivion. I dragged myself into full consciousness and when the Russians began to say something which seemed to me to be of some consequence I stabbed General Hollis wide awake and he passed on the sharp compliment to General Pug. I might just as well have left them in peace. There was nothing of any real moment and this historic occasion droned on to a languid ending. We were all glad to get out into the fresh air.

I have recorded, in the section on Earl Attlee, an account of the Victory Parade on the Charlotten Strasse by British troops. I had time for one other visit to Berlin in company with Brigadier Cornwall-Jones, with whom I had worked closely and much to my profit in my early days in the Joint Planning Staff. He was at this time the Secretary of the Combined Chiefs of Staff. I do not think that either of us felt the slightest twinge of triumph. There was desolation everywhere. We talked in halting phrases to a scarecrow woman who was searching for sticks in the charred remains of the Tiergarten, something to kindle a fire, to hot up a little thin soup for her starving family dwelling in some horrible battered cellar. The streets were masses of rubble, the stench of dead bodies filled the air, the river was full of corpses. These Berliners had paid a heavy price for the short-lived glory of the maniac Führer. More in gratitude for deliverance than in triumph, we visited the Chancellery, saw his study, disordered, chaotic and in ruins. Like any souvenir hunter I pocketed a small piece of marble from the top of his desk, a fragment of his map of the world and a handful of trumpery medals from scattered heaps upon the floor. We saw the bunker in which he had spent his last hectic days and crowned his satanic work with self-slaughter.

In all this desolation there were *boîtes de nuit* of a somewhat sordid kind, hidden away in damp and dirty basements, offering the usual flesh-pots at grossly inflated prices. Nothing was safe or wholesome. The joys, to say the least, were bitter sweet and there was much huckstering and bargaining in black-market commodities. This was an evil shadowy world, inhabited by the human hyenas and jackals who profit by the weakness and miseries of men.

I had no part to play in the political discussions between Churchill (and, subsequently after the General Election, Attlee) and Truman and Stalin; though I was allowed to be present for a brief moment at the start of one of the sessions as the great men assembled. It was interesting enough to watch the delegations arriving at the Cecilienhof. The U.S. President came in an immense cortège, outriders on motor-cycles forming a vanguard, then armoured jeeps, the President's car with G-men crouched on the running-boards, and finally a wagon-load of armed men prepared to give all-round covering fire, the whole proceeding at speed with sirens and whistles blowing importunately. By contrast the British Prime Minister arrived in an unaccompanied private car with a plain-clothes detective on the front seat. 'What is the Russian cortège like?' I enquired of someone. 'When shall we see it? Where does it come from?' 'It doesn't,' I was told. 'There is a puff of smoke and Stalin ascends through the floor.' He did in fact once visit the British delegation area to dine with Churchill and before he descended from his steel bullet-proof car Russian security guards darted out of the accompanying jeeps and formed a human avenue, standing shoulder to shoulder, from the car down a considerable path to the Prime Minister's front door.

As I have already recorded, most of the delegation returned to the United Kingdom for the General Election. In fact most of the military decisions had by then been taken. Accordingly when Attlee and Bevin came back as Britain's representatives they were unaccompanied by the Chiefs of Staff and Service staffs. In consequence I returned at once to London in a Transport Command Dakota which lost its way in a thick cold front just as we seemed about to cross the Channel. An hour or two passed and we flew incessantly in thick cloud. My personal assistant, Miss Harley, and I were about the only passengers. We sat mute in simulated unconcern, but I must confess I was much relieved when an officer came back to reassure us. He admitted with engaging candour that for some time they had not known their whereabouts but now all was well again and we should shortly land at Northolt—which we did.

4

Meeting of Commonwealth Prime Ministers

THE pattern of Commonwealth Prime Ministers' Conferences has changed so radically in recent years that it is
worth trying to recapture the atmosphere and attitudes of these
Conferences in the early fifties when I had the exciting privilege
of attending one or two as Sir Norman Brook's deputy on the
secretariat. In those days—only ten or so years ago—the junior
member was Ceylon. There were no African members except
for the Union, but Southern Rhodesia (not the Central African
Federation, which had not then been called into its uncertain
and faltering existence) attended by a traditional arrangement
as an equal member. With no more than nine members meetings were still possible at No. 10 Downing Street and the
developments and expansion which now make this impossible
have, I am sure, robbed these Conferences of one substantial
point of their mystical significance, without substituting anything comparable in its place. Marlborough House is very fine
—a fine house, originally built by England's greatest architect
for one of England's greatest soldiers, later a royal palace which
has been the gracious residence of many members of the royal
family and has watched over courtly ceremonies and elegant
living—but it has not seen the making of history. No. 10

Downing Street, gimcrack, jerry-built, inconvenient, is yet one of the best-known addresses in the world, the official home of British Prime Ministers for more than two hundred years and the usual meeting place for British Cabinets over the same period. In that Cabinet room great decisions have been taken, great issues debated, high policy made. I grew to know it very well, spent hours of my life in it, noting personalities great and small, patiently listening to wisdom and folly, experiencing excitement and flat boredom. But it never quite lost its enchantment in spite of my familiarity with it. It is a plain enough room, well proportioned, Corinthian columns at one end, two large windows at the other, three windows down one side, the door and fireplace in the wall opposite. The windows look out over a pleasant garden to St. James's Park and the Horse Guards Parade. Most of the available wall space is occupied with bookcases, and over the mantelpiece hangs an indifferent portrait of Sir Robert Walpole, the only picture in the room. Nearly all the floor space is taken up with a large mahogany table covered with green baize cloth, and nineteen or twenty chairs placed around it with some space behind for more chairs for big meetings. It is indeed a small room for a big Conference, but it is a room for intimacy and free exchanges.

In the days of which I am writing, when there were only nine countries attending these Conferences, there was still considerable difficulty and usually a little ill-temper in getting the seating organised in this restricted space. We had to lay down strict rules about attendance—two from each country, that is to say, the Prime Minister and one other (probably the High Commissioner) at the table and two behind. There had to be space for the secretariat and for one or two additional U.K. Ministers, notably the Secretary of State for Commonwealth Relations and the Foreign Secretary who were expected to comment on Commonwealth and international affairs. Some countries found these restrictions on the size of their delegations irksome and there were usually last-minute attempts to gate-crash, which Brook or I had to prevent with what courtesy we could. It can be troublesome and even dangerous in international Conferences to find yourself, without warning, short of the one expert who knows the answers. But Commonwealth Conferences were not like that and a great deal of freedom and candour in exchanging of views was gained by the absence of large numbers of ardent officials all eager to write little notes or whisper advice into the uneasy ear of their Chief.

The seating puzzle did not end with the allocation of the number of seats to each delegation. There remained the juxta-position of the delegations at the table. There is an order of seniority for countries other than the U.K. and in the days of which I am writing Canada was first and Ceylon last. This order of seniority might have served as the protocol for seating, but it had the, at this time, rather unfortunate result of placing India between South Africa and Pakistan. This would not have been a very tactful arrangement and we decided that by placing Canada opposite the U.K. we had done enough to satisfy protocol. For the rest, we seated delegations where we thought they would be most at ease.

Naturally there was much activity for many weeks before one of these Conferences could begin. The first step was the communication to other Commonwealth countries of the proposal to hold a Conference, followed by the extremely difficult task of finding a date at which all Prime Ministers could attend. Not only are they very busy men in their own countries, with urgent domestic problems and their own Parliaments to serve and to consider, but there are international meetings, sessions of the United Nations and so on. Once the date was settled, a choice was made of subjects for discussion— wide and comprehensive subjects covering the whole world. This was not an Agenda, since it was not expected that particular decisions would be taken on particular subjects.

They were simply subjects for discussion and for exchange of views. Briefs had then to be prepared on all these subjects from which the U.K. Prime Minister and other Ministers could speak. This involved much labour and foresight—the explanation of our own attitude and a prophecy of the attitude likely to be adopted by the others—much guidance from Sir Percivale Liesching, then the Permanent Secretary at the Commonwealth Relations Office, much consultation between departments, much telegraphing back and forth to High Commissioners. The Cabinet Office usually made itself responsible for seeing that all briefs were prepared on time and that all the ground had been covered.

As we went through all these laborious preliminaries—additional of course to the normal run of work—I found my excitement increasing—more perhaps on the first occasion than on subsequent ones. Things worked up to a climax. There was the usual last-minute rush, nagging some overworked officials to get a brief prepared on time, jockeying with a thousand other interests to get Ministers to meet and consider the briefs and give them their blessing, answering a multitude of questions from Commonwealth houses in London, organising the times and methods of the secretariat, working very late hours, trying to contain nervous irritation, to condone the negligence of fools and to endure in calm and patience frequent manifestations of temperamental excitability. There is never any lack of officials eager to kick up dust from the cleanest floor and anxious to earn praise and distinction by a continuous display of ostentatious zeal. From Brook I learnt the strength and power of a truly calm, objective and unhurried judgment.

The day before the Conference began we used to hold a meeting in the Cabinet Office of all the leading officials from all the Commonwealth countries. Brook presided and the purpose of the meeting was to discuss and confirm all the administrative arrangements—the times of meetings, the Agenda, the distribution of papers, the security regulations and so on. This meeting was less useful than it sounds. Most of the points had in fact already been agreed with Commonwealth houses in London and owing to the hazards and horrors of air travel it was almost certain that some delegations would not be represented at all. The poor travel-stained officials who did attend were often too tired and heavy-eyed to follow the proceedings. But if we had failed to have the meeting it would have been said in some quarters that as usual the U.K. were trying to boss the whole show and rig the Conference.

The other curtain-raiser to the Conference used to be the official photograph, taken, if fine, in the garden of No. 10 Downing Street. At one time a good many officials managed to find places in the group, but in the years of which I am writing officials were excluded. Ministers alone faced the camera. The passage walls in the Cabinet Office are adorned with copies of these groups, from the earliest days of Imperial Conferences, and the social historian has something to learn from the changing fashions in which Dominion and later Commonwealth Prime Ministers saw fit to clothe themselves.

The stage is now set and the curtain rises on a jostling throng of Ministers and officials clambering round the Cabinet room, chattering with their friends and getting themselves installed. By tradition the U.K. Prime Minister presides, sitting with his back to the fireplace beneath the indifferent portrait of Sir Robert Walpole. In the days of which I am writing the opening sessions of the Conference were devoted to a more or less formal *exposé* by each Prime Minister in turn of his country's view of the international situation in its broadest sense. There was perhaps some lack of warmth and personal appeal about these formal speeches, very often read out from a prepared text, but they had their peculiar interest all the same. To me seeing these visiting Prime Ministers for the first time these lengthy disquisitions offered an opportunity to study closely the manner and appearance of each Prime Minister whether he was speaking or listening. A more disquieting interest was the wide disparity of views expressed. How, I asked myself at the end of these opening sessions, was it possible to pretend that there was any solidarity of opinion in the Commonwealth, any real bond of amity? My high expectations were utterly deflated as I listened in turn to Mr. Nehru and Mr. Liaqat Ali Khan, and how could Dr. Malan fit into the Commonwealth pattern at all?

The subsequent sessions restored my faith and indeed increased it. As the Prime Ministers proceeded to a more detailed examination of particular regions of the world and their particular economic, political and strategic problems, and as the style of the discussion moved from the didactic to the interlocutory, the true significance of the Commonwealth began to reveal itself and to stamp itself on my feelings, so that even now, with South Africa in exile, I cling to my faith in a Commonwealth mystique. It was not that decisions were reached. They were not. It might be said that they were studiously avoided. It was not that internal Commonwealth problems were calmly and dispassionately discussed. They were not discussed at all. On one occasion, it is true, Mr. Menzies tried to mediate from his sickbed in the Savoy Hotel in the Kashmir dispute, but nobody would have dreamt of discussing it in the Cabinet room at No. 10. This may sound weak and feeble and fumbling. How can the Commonwealth be a force in the world if it cannot settle its own disputes and if at the end of its Conference a communiqué of arid, indecisive platitudes is given out to the world?

Agreements and decisions are not the sole purpose of meetings and associations of men and countries. This is a truth that the twentieth century has now begun to learn. A meeting of Heads of Governments is not necessarily a failure because no decision has been taken. Heads of Governments have met and talked together and have separated without taking a decision—not even a wrong one. A great deal has been gained and the

whole point about the Commonwealth is that its members like
meeting and talking to each other. They exchange opinions in
an atmosphere of friendship without any of that unwelcome
spirit of huckstering and bargaining to gain a negotiating point.
The Commonwealth is the only association of free independent
states in the world—in the whole of history, I think—where
there is a real desire and willingness to agree if at all possible.
There is no scoring of points, no deliberate rubbing of sore
spots, no attempt to appeal to the ignorance and prejudice of
the masses behind the backs of the Conference. It must be
widely known by this time that this is by no means the spirit in
which most international Conferences are conducted. Even in
the war Anglo-American Conferences, about which I have
written in another chapter, were far from being consistently
unruffled and harmonious. It might have been thought that in
a war, where the sole object was to win it as soon as possible,
two mighty nations, by providential chance speaking the same
language, would have planned harmoniously together without
suspicion or misunderstanding. This was by no means the case,
as I have freely hinted. It seemed sometimes as if both countries
were deliberately looking for points of disagreement, seeing
bogies and pitfalls in everything, afraid of candour, mistrustful,
revengeful, proud. I have done many negotiations with
Americans during the war and in the years immediately
following it—for the most part easy, friendly and fruitful, but
now and then in an atmosphere so charged with angry suspicion that progress seemed impossible. It is perhaps true that
the British, assuming, with what they hope is an air of modesty,
an attitude of effortless superiority, very soon exasperate their
allies. I have seen it happen in Brussels Treaty days. I have seen
it happen between Commonwealth officials, but I never saw it
or felt it in a meeting of Commonwealth Prime Ministers. On
the contrary they set about their task by searching for points of
agreement. They try to turn a blind eye to bogies and pitfalls.

They speak with disarming candour and in a spirit of concilia-
tion. They are well aware that they are taking part in an experiment and they want it to succeed. That is the key to the position. These Prime Ministers sit down together because they
want to, not because they all hold the same faith and the same
enthusiasms, but because on the whole they like each other's
company and want to get to know each other better. That
after all is what friends do. We like to sit and talk to each other,
almost certainly arguing and disagreeing from time to time,
but without any sort of rancour and in the sure knowledge
that basic affinities and sympathies subsist and that each session
of talk brings us into greater accord and greater affection. That
is how it seemed to me ten years ago and that I believe is still
the atmosphere. The Commonwealth holds together because
the members like it. There is no other association in the world
where they can sit and say what they like, disagreeing with their
friends without losing their friendship, coming to no particular
conclusion without feeling frustrated, and going off to bed with
a genuine wish that the next meeting will come round again
soon.

These were the conclusions I reached after attendance at
these Conferences. While they were in progress, while the
speeches and the arguments proceeded, I was sensitive to strong
impressions of the personalities around me. I have seen both
Churchill and Attlee preside at these meetings, each in his
individual style. I have said enough in another chapter to
suggest what this style was. Attlee, as usual, was business-like,
sensible and liberal, but unable to bring any colour and warmth
into his approach. He was courteous, of course, but distant,
graceless; afraid, it seemed to me, to let himself go. In fact he
was closely responsible for the scene I am trying to describe. It
was his actions, his decisions, his determination, which had
brought India and Pakistan to that table as equal partners with
the old Dominions. It was, of course, part of his Socialist creed

to include all coloured men in his somewhat frigid embrace. As I have said elsewhere, he was never European-minded and I do not think he had any love for yellow men.

Churchill, on the other hand, who would I suspect secretly have preferred to restrict the Commonwealth to the old Dominions, was expansive, graceful, humorous, determined to bring this new Commonwealth within the ambit of his charm and to make the new countries feel the full strength and scope of British prestige. He never failed to bring the human touch into any gathering and I remember that one morning as we assembled at the table he observed opposite to him Mr. Havenga, the South African Finance Minister, sitting next to Dr. Malan. Mr. Havenga had fought against us in the South African war and been many times wounded. 'There he is,' said Winston beaming across the table, 'there he is, you see, full of British bullets and no animosity.'

With these two British Prime Ministers I have seen two British Foreign Secretaries—Ernest Bevin and Anthony Eden—playing their parts in these Conferences. These two men were as sharply contrasted as their chiefs, but in opposite directions. Ernie Bevin had the warmth and colour, Anthony Eden the masterly efficiency. My recollection of Uncle Ernie in this connection is, however, of a man clearly past his best. The random wisdom, often hard to comprehend, which had enabled him to dominate his Brussels Treaty colleagues was gradually disappearing into a more and more confused articulation and periods of physical strain, when he would sit, hardly attentive now, with pendulous stomach and great head lolling upon his chest. It is painful to me to recall the physical decline of this great man, who shared with Churchill a brave, magnanimous, enduring heart and an abundant faith in the future of the British race. Enough of this still shone out, as the clouds cleared suddenly from his weary head, to make the Commonwealth Prime Ministers feel that, so long as Bevin lived, the influence of the U.K. in world affairs would suffer no decline. Anthony Eden, by contrast, was smooth, immaculate, alert, a master of his subject, lucid, attentive, quick in understanding and quick in reply; but even then both appreciation and judgment seemed too closely linked with the pretensions of the person.

As I think of other figures seated round the table in those days, I have a picture in my mind of Mr. Senanayake the first Prime Minister of an independent Ceylon, spontaneously creating around him an atmosphere of benevolence and wisdom. His command of English, or at any rate of a recognizable English accent, was so imperfect that we in the secretariat had very great difficulty in recording his oracular statements. My recollection of Liaqat Ali Khan is superficial and fragmentary. He first refused to attend at all, because, not for the first or last time, he felt too angry with Mr. Nehru to sit at the same table with him. When at last he was persuaded that thorny subjects like Kashmir would not be discussed, he swallowed his bitterness, put in a somewhat belated appearance and behaved courteously with suave self-control. A somewhat severe and taciturn figure at the table was Mr. St. Laurent, the Prime Minister of Canada. He had a composed and trim dignity. His emotions were at all times firmly under control and his interventions into the discussion were brief and wholly unrhetorical. There was nevertheless a certain magnetism about his unruffled courtesy and, although he never seemed quite at home with us, his remarks were crisp and to the point and were particularly valuable to us because of their transatlantic connotations. It fell to him, as Prime Minister of the senior Commonwealth country, to propose, in the final session, a vote of thanks to the U.K. as the host Government. This small ceremonial task he performed with dignity, but with some relief, I felt—unlike the others—that the meetings were now concluded.

The Union of South Africa was, of course, in those days still a member—and an old-established one—of the Commonwealth

K

and at the meetings I have in the forefront of my memory was represented by Dr. Malan, the Prime Minister,
and Mr. Havenga, the Finance Minister. Even then the South
African representatives seemed isolated, following domestic
policies which nobody else at that table—with the possible
exception of Godfrey Huggins—could have approved. These
issues were not discussed, as I have explained, any more than
Kashmir, but in any discussion of the cold war, of anti-
Communist policies, Dr. Malan was positive and enthusiastic.
A large, coarse-looking man, speaking English in the clipped
unfinished accents of the Dutch-speaking South African, he
was more courteous, more friendly to us, more inclined
towards the Commonwealth, than his public utterances and
attitudes would have led us to expect. I felt then, as I feel now,
that the defection of South Africa would be dangerous—
dangerous to the South African Government because there
would be no restraining hand, no liberalising influence—
dangerous to the Commonwealth because it would become
clear that generous embrace after conquest or tutelage led to
no enduring and affectionate relationship.

By contrast a straightforward figure, whose position on
every subject could be safely predicted, was Sidney Holland, at
that time Prime Minister of New Zealand. It was at these meetings that I first saw him and I have attempted to give a picture
of him elsewhere. He spoke without subtlety or finesse, anxious
only to express the two uppermost feelings in his head—
loyalty to the U.K. and friendship to the United States. He
pursued one object and one only throughout his first Conference. He wanted the Prime Ministers assembled to send a joint
message of cordial friendship and co-operation to the United
States—a suggestion which did not commend itself to Mr. Nehru
and had to be tacitly dropped. But Mr. Holland was easy to understand and after the tortuous and labyrinthine arguments of
some Prime Ministers his was a clear and refreshing voice.

A prominent statesman among this number at this time—and since—was Mr. Menzies, who has attained something like the international status of General Smuts in his later years. He was prepared to talk on every subject—and he talked well and liberally. He made a conscious and sustained effort to understand the differing points of view around the table and to find meeting points between them. I think he did more than any man in these years to reconcile the divergent feelings of the old and the new Commonwealth on international affairs. Even Mr. Nehru, then in the early brightness of his uncommitted neutralism, was not unwilling to listen to the persuasive tongue of this clever Australian. But for the most part, I think, Mr. Nehru enjoyed the sound of his own voice—and so did I. His charm was compelling. He spoke at length, with a rich fluency —better English than anyone in the room, not excluding Churchill. He argued, he maintained, he refined, he wondered, he puzzled, turning aside into an intriguing byway, returning to the main road, slipping off again and returning once more. He wove spells and charms around you, but when it was done nobody—not even Mr. Nehru himself—was quite sure what it really amounted to.

The Prime Minister of Southern Rhodesia, Sir Godfrey Huggins, was less attracted by these lengthy discourses than I was. As is well known, Sir Godfrey is deaf and wears a hearing aid, but like all men in this situation when his aid is not in operation he has no idea how loud his own voice is. For a long time he listened patiently, with his aid in his ear, to one of these complex and tortuous discourses of Mr. Nehru. At length, growing tired, he removed his aid, turned round to me, sitting immediately behind him, and made some uncomplimentary remarks in stentorian and ringing tones. The whole room heard them and pretended not to. I made a silent, non-committal smile and Mr. Nehru continued, unchecked and unashamed.

The closing scenes of these meetings included the drafting of

the communiqué and its final approval by the Prime Ministers.
This operation was not without its trials. To some extent it was
prefabricated. It had to follow certain conventional and well-
established lines. It could not say anything very decisive or
constructive—because as I have tried to explain that is not really
what these meetings were about. It was our custom therefore
to produce in the Cabinet secretariat a first draft of the
communiqué during the course of the meeting and to lay it
before the committee of Commonwealth officials, appointed
to draw up a communiqué, as a first working draft—something
on which to argue. This usually worked fairly well but sometimes one of the delegations would also without warning
produce a first draft—and then, of course, things became very
confusing. The eager officials would suggest many amend-
ments but it was often not at all clear which of the two drafts
they were trying to amend—and in the end it was usually up to
Brook and me to try to 'marry' the two drafts into a new and
better one. There would then follow a great deal of haggling
and arguing over words and phrases—none of more than
verbal importance. There is nothing men enjoy more than
sitting round a table trying to show that they have a better
command of English than other men. And no one was more
argumentative about words and more tenacious than a very
wise Indian official, Sir Girja Bajpai, now dead, whose knowledge of English was equal to Mr. Nehru's, if not superior.
Well do I remember a communiqué meeting which dragged
on interminably and irritatingly. There was much to do and
the wretched thing had to be got ready and circulated immediately after lunch. Time went on, 1.00 came, 1.30 came and
Bajpai, who was the chief trouble-maker, suddenly said: 'I can
see that many of you are anxious about the time and about your
lunch. I would remind you that I am a Brahmin and that I am
therefore quite able to be interminably disputatious and equally
accustomed to fasting. But I will press the point no further.'

The Prime Ministers usually accepted the communiqué without very much alteration but without enthusiasm. Some wanted more colour and some less and that is just why it was such a hopeless task. The Prime Minister of Canada, on behalf of all the visiting delegations, then thanked the U.K. Prime Minister for his hospitality and for his conduct of the meeting. The delegations clambered and clattered out. The voices died away and Sir Robert Walpole gazed down upon an empty room.

5

The Brussels Treaty—
The Foundation of N.A.T.O.

THE Brussels Treaty was signed on 17th March 1948. The signatories—France, Belgium, the Netherlands, Luxembourg and the United Kingdom—bound themselves, amongst other things, to set up a joint defence organisation. The Treaty was to have some substance. The defence organisation was brought into being at a formal meeting at Lancaster House, attended by the Ministers of Defence of the Five Powers, with their Chiefs of Staff. The French and British eyed each other uneasily. Did the insular British mean business this time? Were the French worth backing? Had they really recovered from 1940? Of course, nobody said anything of this kind. The speeches were fulsome, optimistic, fraternal—delivered by British and French Ministers and Chiefs of Staff, each in his own tongue and hastily and rather badly translated. What had to be done? There must be a '*bilan*', said M. Teitgen, French Minister of Defence at that moment but not for many moments more. What was a '*bilan*'?—a word unknown to Mr. A. V. Alexander, at this time the British Minister of Defence, but surely dangerous and difficult to make such a request so early. But harmony and friendship must be sustained, so a '*bilan*' there had to be. And the '*bilan*' must be drawn up in the '*cadre*' of a

strategy for the '*défense de L'Europe occidentale*'. Of course, of
course; there could be no argument about that. And Field
Marshal Montgomery, the C.I.G.S. at the time, was most eager
that it should be done at once—tomorrow, today, why wait?
But there must be some organisation to think up this strategy
and make this '*bilan*'. Yes, at once, a Military Committee with
one representative from each of the Five Powers, to meet and
work together in London and report to the Chiefs of Staff, all
five sets of them. And they in turn should report to the five
Ministers of Defence. This is capital progress, thought A. V.
Alexander, and to inject an even greater sense of realism and to
gain credit for showing practical initiative he puffed out his
chest to magisterial proportions and proposed in grating tones
that the Military Committee should meet on the following
Tuesday in five days' time. The general sense of satisfaction was
very great. A lone unwelcome voice enquired who the members of the Military Committee should be and where the first
meeting should take place—odious matters of detail, not fit to
engage the attention of Ministers. But at least there must be a
secretary and he could do the rest. With grave magnanimity,
as if parting with his most cherished adviser, Mr. Alexander
offered a British official, whom if he knew at all he somewhat
mistrusted, for this task. Ah! the British again; they wanted to
run the whole show, of course, but no one was ready with a
counter-proposal and I suddenly found myself the secretary of
a non-existent Military Committee under orders to meet in
five days, and to keep on meeting, in a building in London, as
yet not specified.

Well! What a splendid morning's work! And now, as we
have a secretary, he can draft a communiqué and an outline of
the proposals already agreed. We will have lunch and return
afterwards to conclude the proceedings and approve the
communiqué. And by the way, the Americans and Canadians
would like to attend meetings as observers—that must be

worked in somehow. And, of course, there must be two texts, English and French.

I was a little late for lunch. When I did arrive my chair had been removed to give M. Teitgen more elbow room. I tried to withdraw unnoticed from the room, but Robert Johnston, the rotund and bustling Principal Establishment Officer in the Ministry of Defence, would have none of it and with dauntless resolution he manœuvred me back into my rightful place. Heated and embarrassed, I made halting and superficial conversation in execrable French with M. Teitgen whose friendly charm was manifested in his own tongue only.

In an atmosphere of cigar smoke and bonhomie—with a chorus of 'Tray bongs' from Mr. Alexander to show his sincere sense of companionship—the meeting was concluded, but not without an intervention of subtle charm from M. Teitgen, who insisted, as if he were presenting me with a bouquet of flowers, that there should be no reference in the communiqué to the fact that the secretariat was to be in the hands of the British. Out they all went, linking arms, puffing out their chests, mustering up 'au revoirs' and 'goodbyes', and posing for the bemused and patient photographers. I sat and scratched my head. Sir Harold Parker, at that time Permanent Secretary in the Ministry of Defence, has preserved a photograph of this occasion—himself descending the steps of Lancaster House, cigar in mouth, his lean length strangely contrasted with the short jaunty figure of General Hollis in the uniform of a Royal Marines General. The French admitted to me later that they had tried very hard to assess the influence of each of the personalities arrayed before them. They knew about Montgomery, of course, but they had concluded, with misplaced subtlety, that General Hollis was the éminence grise and I was being 'planted' by him as a sort of spy or agent of his in their midst.

The meeting on the following Tuesday did in fact take place. Robert Johnston, pushing, indefatigable, claiming the authority

of the Minister of Defence, swept aside all obstacles and somehow achieved a building—and a building moreover in the very
heart of Whitehall. From the Horse Guards Parade it looked
attractive and imposing, with its fine eighteenth-century façade
in grey stone. This façade had been transported from a house in
Great George Street, demolished to make way for the massive
block of the New Public Offices, and fitted on to an existing
house on Horse Guards. Inside, it did not quite fit, and the
relationship of rooms and windows was odd and inconvenient
but not unattractive. The real drawback to the house was that
only half of it remained; it was only one room thick. The back
of the house facing Whitehall had been severely bombed and
remained an ugly unusable chaos. But it was a building. It was
somewhere to begin this strange adventure—five European
Powers with a joint defence organisation, development as yet
unheard of in the history of Europe.

By what ingenuity of clerical and secretarial devices the
Military Committee was nominated, summoned and furnished
with the necessary documents in two languages for its first
meeting is the fevered tale of a lost weekend and not now
worth the effort to remember. Robert Johnston provided me
with the minimum staff for my hectic needs—as if he were
conjuring rabbits from a hat—and they were all of the first
class, my cheerful, friendly, loyal helpers.

The meeting was summoned for 3 p.m. on that fatal Tuesday
at No. 36 Whitehall—entrance on the Horse Guards Parade,
a necessary warning because the entrance on Whitehall was
squalid and virtually useless since it offered access only to rooms
of distorted and disordered masses of rubble. The entrance on
Horse Guards was attractive and immediately on the right of it
was the conference room, well proportioned, rectangular,
with its original panelling and large windows looking out across
the parade ground to the trees of St. James's Park. A good
mahogany table and chairs were in position and there was room

behind these for the overflow of staffs. I experienced some inward nervous tension as the hour approached, but this found outlet in laughter as I entered the conference room fifteen minutes before the appointed hour. The tables and chairs were in some disarray, the documents so painstakingly produced not yet distributed, two or three electricians crawling about the floor fixing the lights, the chief clerk vainly trying to hurry them up, wringing his hands and performing little pirouetting turns about the room, other clerks struggling to distribute the papers in the proper places, two agitated interpreters begging for clearer instructions. Into this turmoil the delegations began to arrive, four or five officers in each delegation, but only one from little Luxembourg. Nobody knew anybody else and only one or two could speak any language but his own. The confusion seemed impenetrable, but it was good-humoured and it gradually sorted itself out in an exchange of wordless smiles. At last the electricians were dragged up from the floor and ejected, the traffic at the door ceased, the delegations, tripping over chairs, elbowed their way into their appointed places and the meeting began. As hosts the United Kingdom took the Chair and Air Vice-Marshal Hudleston, young, fair-haired, blue-eyed, looking unutterably Anglo-Saxon, presided with a sort of benign and boyish charm. At this time he knew hardly a word of French and he has never been fluent or loquacious even in his own tongue, but his somewhat halting utterances were a great advantage on this occasion, as the borrowed interpreters, nobly struggling with subjects quite unknown to them, had more time to invent circumlocutions which might possibly give the right idea of the technical jargon in which for the most part he spoke. The other delegations expressed their views briefly upon the various items and documents which, in the short time available, I had managed to present to them—General Doorman, the Netherlands representative, easy-going, friendly, full of common sense; General Deleval, the Belgian, alive with good nature, voluble in an accent almost incomprehensible to French ears; Major Albrecht, from Luxembourg, shy to find himself representing his country in a committee of Generals; General Ely, austere, ascetic, delicate, sensitive, made comments of penetrating intelligence; General Kibler, the United States observer, looking I thought like a relic of the Civil War; and General Clark, the Canadian observer, who found himself in the press and overcrowding relegated to a table behind the main one—a decision of mine which had for a short time unpleasant consequences. These, then, were the men with whom I was to work for two years and already at that first meeting their characters and personalities began to manifest themselves —good, loyal men affectionately remembered for themselves and for their work.

In that bombed-out house we stayed and worked for a good many months, getting ourselves established, making our unaccustomed presence better known, working out the basis of our Five-Power co-operation, adding up our resources, trying to convince the Chiefs of Staff and Ministers of Defence above us that this was an effective alliance and that it had some substance and strength. We groped and stumbled sometimes. The Canadian High Commissioner—Mr. Norman Robertson— called on me in person to protest against my affront to General Clark in putting him at the back at that first meeting. Was this the way for one Commonwealth country to treat another? In my present job, I explained, I was not British. In serving Five Powers I belonged to all and not to one. What should I have done in setting that table? There was not room for all. I could not displace one of the signatories—no, not even Luxembourg, an equal sovereign power. It had to be the United States or Canada. In my denationalised and objective state I had chosen to displace the less powerful of these two. Norman Robertson was vexed, unable to comprehend such a novel notion of a British official unbritishised. But he accepted the explanation and Fin Clark and I became firm friends.

For a few weeks we sailed on calmly, putting up with the inconveniences of that strange house, trying to like each other and succeeding in the main. There came a day when Ted Hudleston had to put over to his colleagues what seemed a severe decision of the British Chiefs of Staff. He did it, abruptly and peremptorily, and as the translation of his terse sentences beat upon the ears of General Ely, his white ascetic face became more white and more severe, his eyes lost their light, his mouth closed tight and thin. He was startled into stone. His reply, when it came, was equally terse, equally uncompromising, and my sleep was troubled with fears for the health and survival of this infant organisation. But it survived that check and a good many more severe that followed. There was friendship between these two men and a deep respect. They could not speak to each other except through interpreters, but they needed no words or language to appreciate and approve each other's sterling qualities. Inevitably they took the lead in our deliberations and their mutual respect and understanding were the sinews of our strength.

One paramount object of the British Chiefs of Staff was to set up a Command organisation, Commanders-in-Chief and their Headquarters, to give practical point to all our paper plans. This led to much argument and much mistrust. Who was to be the Supreme Commander? It could not be an American, because the United States were not signatories of the Treaty. The French were not at all anxious to subordinate themselves to the British and the British continued to maintain that no French General, since the débâcle of 1940, had sufficient experience of modern war. Let there be, then, a committee of three Commanders-in-Chief, Land, Air and Sea, with an additional and independent Chairman. This compromise took a deal of hammering out and led in the result to many tears.

The French were lukewarm and very hesitant about it. The

British became insistent and peremptory and one memorable evening Mr. A. V. Alexander summoned General Ely to his room in the Ministry of Defence and delivered an ultimatum, roughly and rudely presented. General Ely, who was suffering from influenza, sat white and still and inwardly angry, but undertook there and then to leave for Paris and come back in two days with a satisfactory response. Mr. Alexander was delighted and his ill-tempered rudeness changed in a trice to a loquacious and incoherent bonhomie. Stories were told, incidents recalled, all designed to reassure the French; and to please and impress this intellectual and sensitive General quotations were dragged in to illustrate and illuminate. One of these went astray in the middle. What was it now? Something from the 'Lady of Shalott', Mr. Alexander thought; and a private secretary went scurrying from the room in an excess of zeal, only to return with a copy of the works of Walter Scott. General Ely sat amazed and withdrawn. He was feeling very ill. He wanted only to catch his aeroplane and tackle his difficult task in Paris. But he realised that this strange and somewhat ludicrous scene was intended as a manifestation of friendliness and he managed somehow to conjure up friendly smiles and to conceal his impatience.

I walked back with him across the Horse Guards Parade, trying to explain the strange and awkward angles of the Anglo-Saxon temperament and mentality, and delivered him to his anxious and devoted staff, who bundled him, ill and shivering but not in the least agitated or angry, into a car and drove him off to the airport. He accomplished his mission—by stratagems and devices, which he recounted to me years later, and with the ruthless tenacity of which this gentle man is capable. The result was that a full-dress meeting of the five Ministers of Defence in Paris followed as soon as I could organize it. Its purpose was to approve the proposed Committee of Commanders-in-Chief and to nominate the members. When some less important business had been concluded in plenary session M. Ramadier, then French Minister of Defence, proposed that the main and confidential business should be handled in restricted session with nobody present but the Ministers themselves. I had had experience of this sort of thing before. Each Minister would have his own version of the discussion and there would be no clear-cut decision on which to initiate action. Moreover, M. Ramadier could speak no English and Mr. Alexander no French. If there was to be any controversy it would be between these two men. Although they were both Socialists of much the same vintage and had doubtless exchanged the usual fraternal greetings at many international Conferences, there seemed to be little love lost between them—Mr. Alexander strutting and posing as authoritative and imperious, M. Ramadier a bearded intellectual but tenacious and combative when required. I have noticed that for all their international protestations Socialist politicians from different countries love each other much less than Conservatives. In these circumstances I thought it unlikely that they would ever make themselves clear to each other. I suggested, therefore, that an interpreter and I should be admitted to the discussion. M. Ramadier was reluctant, perhaps still a little suspicious that I would merely add weight to the British case. I pressed the point hard. I could foresee most unhappy consequences unless there were an impartial account of the discussion and a clearly defined decision. He finally met me in an illogical spirit of compromise. He would admit me but no interpreter; I must do the interpreting. This was an unexpected shock; for, though my understanding of French was adequate, my expression was imperfect and hesitant. But I was not going to lose what I had gained by inappropriate modesty or cowardice. As it turned out the meeting was not difficult—General Ely had prepared the ground—and with the aid of Colonel de Fraiteur, the Belgian Minister, who spoke English, we got through and the Committee of Commanders-in-Chief came into being—Field Marshal Montgomery himself as the independent Chairman, General de Lattre de Tassigny as the Land Commander-in-Chief, Air Marshal Robb as the Air Commander-in-Chief and Admiral Jaujard as the Naval Adviser—at that stage names only to me, great names and great reputations. I had never seen General de Lattre. The great Field Marshal Montgomery, whose repute in this year of 1948 was still resounding through the world, I had seen often and studied at fairly close quarters but from the worm's-eye view only. I was not known to him personally and I had not served in the 8th Army.

I returned from this momentous conference in the night ferry with my personal staff—Mr. West, my chief clerk, Miss Harley, my personal assistant, and Captain Chandler and Flight Lieutenant Baxter, my interpreters. Mr. Alexander and the United Kingdom delegation had intended to return by the same train, but at the last minute their plans were altered and their reservations cancelled. As we pulled in to Victoria Station in the early morning I was standing at the carriage window, untidy and unshaven (as I intended to go straight home), when I observed the station-master in full fig, tails and top hat, waiting upon the platform. I realized at once that he had not been warned and that he had come dutifully out to meet the British Minister of Defence. My carriage stopped just by him. Hastily I said: 'Mr. Alexander is not on the train, after all. Don't be upset. Meet me instead. I am an international civil servant.' Quickly and roughly I outlined my status. He can have had no idea who or what I was, but he liked my cheek and my humour and he acquiesced. I assembled my little team, astonished and delighted. Ceremoniously we descended on to the platform. Solemnly I shook the station-master's hand and courteously he led us past the little knot of inquisitive people, who always gather on such occasions, through the Customs and on to the waiting cars.

Much activity followed from the decision in Paris. Buildings for Headquarters had to be commandeered, a part of the Palace of Fontainebleau for the three Commanders-in-Chief and Dover House, just the other side of the Horse Guards arch from us, as the rear Headquarters for the Field Marshal; staffs had to be assembled, staffs of mixed nationalities, to mark the idea of Western European co-operation, Western Union; a château, the main wing of the Château de Courances, near Fontainebleau, was provided by private generosity and the courtesy of the French Government as a residence for the Field Marshal; and Great Britain had to find a new C.I.G.S. With far-seeing wisdom Mr. Attlee fetched back General Sir William Slim from the Railway Executive.

When the new organisation had been in operation for a few months it was felt that this Committee of Commanders-in-Chief should come and give an account of their stewardship to the Chiefs of Staff of the Five Powers (known as the Western Union Chiefs of Staff Committee) who were their titular masters. It was widely known that the path of progress had not been altogether smooth, but I was not prepared for the shocks and the confusion which attended the meeting between them so carefully organised at No. 36 Whitehall. In that same room, where our original meeting had taken place some six months earlier, these great military leaders assembled. If they had been opera-singers we should have had an easier day. Lord Tedder, then Chairman of the United Kingdom Chiefs of Staff, took the Chair, and he had ranged on each side of him the Chiefs of Staff from the other Four Powers, including General Lechères, at that time Chairman of the French Chiefs of Staff. Opposite to Tedder was the great Field Marshal and at each end of the table General de Lattre and Air Marshal Robb. The great men got themselves seated without any untoward incident—unusual this, as the seating of the great, whether at meetings or at social functions, is a matter of the utmost delicacy about which serious

books have been written. I had already suffered one rebuff, but
this time, I thought, at least that particular hurdle had been
jumped. It was not at all difficult to feel the chill in the temperature as we took our seats. There was never any love lost
between Tedder and Monty, and this occasion, on which
Tedder was on the superior level receiving a report submitted
by Monty, was not calculated to bring out any display of grace
or courtesy from Monty—if indeed there is any grace in his
make-up. From the moment we entered the room it was clear
that General de Lattre was in a sulk, his natural charm and
smile deliberately obliterated by an ill-tempered pout. The
clouds were piling up menacingly; there was certain to be an
explosion. Tedder's impish humour is usually attracted by this
sort of situation. He plays with it. He gets in sly digs and
malicious witticisms and provokes his opponents into foolish
anger, thus weakening their case. But that, he felt, rightly, was
not the appropriate mood for that day. Too much was at stake.
The foundations of our alliance were too insecure. The danger,
against which we were the only rather feeble bastion, was too
insistent. Tedder played his part quietly and humorously—
though I judged that the humour was lost on everyone in the
room but me, and my mouth was too dry with nervous
apprehension to offer much of a smile. I do not now remember
the course of the argument. It mattered much at the time but it
has been swallowed up long since in events and practical
results. The Field Marshal was, I think, giving his account of the
working of the Commanders-in-Chief Committee, speaking
on behalf of all of them and doing it in his usual jerky, succinct
fashion. He had just entered upon the subject of the land
forces when General de Lattre made an ill-tempered intervention. His general thesis was that he was the Commander-in-
Chief Land Forces and that the Field Marshal, as chairman of a
committee, had no direct responsibility for them and should
keep his finger out of that pie. The exchanges grew somewhat

L

heated and the interpreters had a very uncomfortable time. General de Lattre was free with '*J'insiste*' and '*Je demande*' and these, when hastily interpreted as 'I insist' and 'I demand', roused the wrath of the Field Marshal. The only way out of this unseemly argument was to adjourn the meeting in order that the Western Union Chiefs of Staff might reconsider the wording of the directive which had been given to the Commanders-in-Chief Committee, and this course Tedder adopted. The Field Marshal and the Commanders-in-Chief withdrew, red and ruffled, escaping from each other, I have no doubt, as quickly as they left the building. Lord Tedder, General Lechères and I retired to my room to scratch our heads and find a solution. There was no solution—there never is to the antipathy of two strong men. But we found some means of papering over the cracks and preventing the dissolution of the Commanders-in-Chief organisation. I do not now remember how the day proceeded from then or how exactly it ended. There was the usual browbeating from the Field Marshal—'It is up to you to decide. You make the decision, but it must be a clear decision,' and so on—as if the decision were perfectly simple and would be loyally carried out by all concerned without any damage whatever to the alliance. The Field Marshal has a passion for decisions and would, it sometimes seemed, rather have the wrong one than none at all. He even favoured unnecessary decisions—decisions when there was nothing to decide. He used to advise me to take fifteen decisions a day, as if he were prescribing a course of pills. At any rate a decision of a kind was arrived at and the meeting ended, at bitter last, with blank unfriendly protestations of loyalty and co-operation. It was already perfectly clear that what did happen would happen. The work of the staffs would proceed effectively and co-operatively. The antipathy of the Field Marshal and General de Lattre would increase. This was something we would have to live with, and so long as there was no war, and we kept our sense of humour, it did not really matter very much. But it took some living with.

That was a bitter day, but somehow I think we managed to prevent a repetition of this particular form of meeting—the personal confrontation of the Western Union Chiefs of Staff and the Commanders-in-Chief Committee. It could never work. Even if the Commanders-in-Chief had been in harmony and agreement it would have been galling to them to have to report in person to officers who, with the exception of the United Kingdom representative, were of inferior rank and repute to themselves. Of the Five Powers only the United Kingdom had fully developed the idea that the Chief of Staff of each arm of the Service is also the head of that arm. In France the Chief of Staff of the Army was no more than a prominent staff officer and a long way below the level of a Commander-in-Chief like General de Lattre. Reporting on paper was acceptable and the Western Union Chiefs of Staff considered many reports from the Commanders-in-Chief Committee before submitting them with comments to the Ministers of Defence.

The meetings of the five Ministers of Defence, which took place every three or four months in the five capitals in turn, never achieved this level of tension and ill-temper. On the whole they were rather pleasant occasions, partly no doubt because the Ministers of Defence had little more power than power to recommend courses of action to the five Foreign Ministers who were the top layer of the Treaty. I only remember one serious disagreement at these meetings. It occurred at Brussels, but I do not precisely remember what it was about. I remember it because it did threaten a serious rupture in the rhythm of our work. As usual the controversy, such as it was, arose between the British and French, and the first day of the Conference ended with Mr. Alexander and M. Ramadier mistrusting and disliking each other to what seemed to me a quite unnecessary and somewhat infantile degree. I thought I knew a satisfactory way to reconcile their views and to build a bridge strong enough to allow their politically suspicious minds to meet each other. This sort of thing is the real work of a secretariat. The secretary of a committee, especially of a high-level Committee of Ministers, has a constructive duty to perform. It is not enough that he should simply organise meetings and record decisions. If he is not more awake and alert and inventive than that he will not find so very many decisions to record. He has certain advantages over the members of the committee. He alone listens throughout. He may not speak, except in occasional undertones to the chairman. He can listen and concentrate. All the members are thinking what they themselves want to say and their faculties are centred upon the opportunity to say it. They are not really listening to anybody else and even when two members find themselves locked in argument they are concerned more with brandishing effective weapons of abuse than with listening to each other's reasoning. The secretary need not worry his head about the abuse. He must listen and think. He must try to see the true meaning beneath the silly angry words and often he will find that in truth there is no fundamental disagreement and that an initial misunderstanding of meaning has been magnified into a factitious quarrel. He must then play for time and propose a solution privately after the meeting when tempers have cooled. Accordingly I first propounded my solution to Jean-Louis de Rougemont, a French Colonel on my staff, who faithfully and loyally attended me at all these Conferences. He brought his quick intelligence and wit to play upon my scheme and concluded that it was correct and acceptable. But he went further and insisted that it was my duty to put my scheme personally and privately to M. Ramadier during the course of the evening. I was reluctant. I was tired and a little dispirited and I wanted to enjoy the hospitality of the Belgian Government, who were giving an official dinner for us in traditional and lavish style, without any professional brake upon my conviviality. My sense of duty prevailed and after the dinner I found an opportunity to sit down beside M. Ramadier on a sofa. I felt awkward and uncomfortable. Although there was something rather likable about him, he was not attractive, with his little beard and his scruffy untidy clothes and a distinct aroma of cheese about him. He needed some coaxing. He was still feeling sore and angry at Mr. Alexander's rudeness, and I, after all, whatever my protestations of impartiality, was just another of those domineering Britanniques. But he listened and he expressed himself as ready to adopt my suggestion. While we were thus awkwardly juxtaposed upon this sofa, I was conscious, not only of a mocking and amused approval from de Rougemont, but of a baleful glare from Mr. Alexander, who was strutting about the room with a whisky and soda in his hand. He was evidently deeply suspicious of my unseemly flirtation with his enemy. My task of reconciliation was clearly not yet over and when I managed politely to extract myself from the embrace of the Barbichu, I had to board the dreadnought Alexander. His suspicion—and I think dislike—of me was very strong, but his own staff successfully pressed my solution upon him and the next day the Conference proceeded without unmannerly hitch.

The periodic meetings of Western Union Chiefs of Staff, without the Commanders-in-Chief, were in the main harmonious and friendly occasions. Inevitably the British were slightly dominating because they were always represented by one of the three Chiefs of Staff—Lord Tedder or Lord Fraser of North Cape or Sir William Slim, three world-famous names, and each, as I have explained, the acknowledged head of his own Service. But if they were dominating by repute and position they were never domineering, and it was fortunate indeed, in these somewhat brittle days, that the British representatives were men not only of proved ability but of great natural

charm and friendliness. For the French, General Lechères kept
his end up well and if any count could be made of the number
of words spoken at these meetings by each member of the
Western Union Chiefs of Staff he would be an easy winner. He
was most friendly and cheerful and assiduous to advance the
French point of view on every single point. This he did in
speeches of inordinate length and tortuous complexity,
delivered at great speed in a Parisian accent. He was the despair
of the interpreters and sometimes also of General Ely, who sat
anxiously behind him hoping against hope that his verbosity
would not obscure the perfectly valid point which the French
wanted to make. But General Lechères was enthusiastic and
constructive and, though perhaps he strained our patience
sometimes, his contributions were valuable and helpful and I
personally owed much to his friendliness and his sense of
humour and of fun.

Both in and out of school these Western Union Chiefs of
Staff got on with each other, as most military men will. A
professional bond unites them. Language was the only obstacle
to their conviviality; for, though all were eager to insist that all
officers serving in the organisation must speak both French and
English, they themselves remained obstinately monoglot. With
so many other responsibilities on their shoulders they can
hardly be blamed for that. At parties, therefore, a good deal of
extra work fell upon those of us who could make a shot at
both languages. I shall not forget an agonising lunch at which
I sat between Lord Tedder and General Lechères, both in high
good humour, and demanding that I should interpret their
witticisms and funny stories to each other. While I could
understand Lord Tedder's impish idiom I had no idea of the
French equivalent. General Lechères' swift and equally idio-
matic sallies I could not even understand. Lord Tedder was a
constant delight to the French, though it took them some time
to understand his particular form of naughty humour. At a

party in the early days at which he was acting as host he played one of his tricks on me. As I was announced and came forward into the throng of Allied officers to shake his hand, he ostentatiously turned his back on me, saying something like: 'Good heavens! I'm not expected to shake hands with that fellow, am I?' This manœuvre did not pass unobserved and it was felt, I believe, that I had fallen out of favour with the Britanniques. Perhaps it helped my claims to impartiality.

In the later Western Union Chiefs of Staff meetings the British Chiefs of Staff were accompanied by Air Chief Marshal Sir William Elliot, who had replaced General Hollis as Chief Staff Officer to the Minister of Defence. I think he enjoyed these contacts with other European officers and Ministers. He was at ease and his languid charm seemed appropriate in French salons. He spoke French well, with a very un-English accent, careful, elaborate, measured. This talented man is one whose rate of utterance in any language has never quite matched his flow of ideas. Those of us who knew him well and worked a lot with him were able to pick up the idea long before it had been given its polished form in long well-modulated phrases; and it saved a lot of time to leave him, draped elegantly over a chair, in the midst of the labour of oral composition, and go and get on with the job. When he himself set pen to paper, when the act of writing obliged him to match his words to his ideas, the results were remarkable. His private letters were monuments of elegance, not only in the style and choice of words, but in the penmanship itself. The charm and grace had their rough side too and well do I remember a French General, whose name I have forgotten, explaining to me at one of these meetings that he was the French equivalent of Elliot. Elliot happened to overhear this and, as he regarded this particular General with something like contempt, he went to great pains to put him in his place. Claims and counter-claims were bandied about and Elliot was much too busy searching for effective French phrases to listen to the poor man's explanations. I edged away, hoping that the announcement of lunch would put an end to this strange and rather unseemly encounter.

These Conferences, whether of Western Union Chiefs of Staff or of the Ministers of Defence, were staging posts in the progress of our work. The work of the staffs proceeded continuously. In the Headquarters of the Commanders-in-Chief operational and administrative plans to meet various contingencies were hammered out; and in the central organisation controlled by the Military Committee in London efforts were made to achieve common strategic doctrines, common procedures and organisation and common, or at least interchangeable, weapons. In London the work went on in Five-Power committees, each of which was served as secretary by a member of my Five-Power staff. My deputy, Colonel J. Fauchon de Villeplée, of the French Army, had the general responsibility of looking after all these lower-level committees, and he was assisted by Lieutenant-Colonel R. E. Gabbett, a sapper. These two men went about their unusual and delicate duties with great industry and good humour and even gatherings of Five-Power meteorologists, who spoke in an esoteric jargon, did not dismay them. All was faithfully recorded and appropriate action initiated.

With the signing of the North Atlantic Treaty on 4th April 1949 it was clear that our days as an independent organisation were numbered and that we should be gradually absorbed into a much larger and much more comprehensive organisation, in which the Americans would play an active and prominent role. Wisely our work was not ignored and what we had accomplished in our two years of independent existence—the practical results of our co-operation and the goodwill and friendliness of our daily work—became the foundation of N.A.T.O. The mustard seed, planted in April 1948, was growing well.

A Day With
Field Marshal Montgomery

To me personally the Field Marshal was invariably polite and considerate. He knew that I was engaged in a rather delicate juggling act, trying to keep five balls in the air at the same time. He knew that I had fifteen different masters, five on the Military Committee, five on the Western Union Chiefs of Staff Committee and five Ministers of Defence. He detested and despised this cumbersome machinery. He would have swept the whole thing away, if he could have, and me with it. But, as it had to be, it was important that I should be encouraged, sometimes teased and occasionally bullied, to make it work as quickly and effectively as possible. He knew also that in my central position I was the recipient of a good many confidences from all five countries and that I might sometimes be able to throw a fresh light on some of our problems. In consequence he was open with me and occasionally invited me to come and see him alone to discuss either particular or general points. On the first of these occasions I learnt a new technique for interviews—but one which my own soft temperament has never been able to put to use. Things were not going smoothly between him and the French, in particular General de Lattre. What did I think about it? Had I any suggestions or criticisms to make? Yes, I had; but could I be quite frank? 'Of course, of course,' he said, 'that is just what I want.' I had never before been invited to speak with critical candour to a British Field Marshal and I embarked somewhat nervously, wondering how far I should be allowed to go, how soon he would silence me with terse authority. But no interruption came—no interruption at all. As I concluded my first point, I waited for assent or dissent or argument or acknowledgment of some kind, but not a single word was said. Silence reigned until I had summoned up courage to make my next point. Silence again. This was treatment I had not expected but, as there was no signal that I should stop, I went on and on, with dwindling confidence and drier and drier mouth, until I had said all I wanted. 'Thank you,' he said, quite politely, but that was all, and I was glad to get out of the door. I had no idea what effect, if any, my words had produced on him. Did he attach any weight to my opinions? Would he act on any of my suggestions? Was he resentful and angry at my boldness? I had no idea whatever. If he felt any resentment he never showed it and not long after I was invited to go and stay a night with him at Courances, his château near Fontainebleau.

I accompanied him and some members of his personal staff in his private aeroplane, which was, if I remember rightly, a specially fitted Dakota, and we landed at Orly on a beautiful summer day. There was the usual crowd of sightseers at the air-port watching the aeroplanes come and go, but the Field Marshal seemed to assume that they had all turned out to greet him. He walked across the tarmac to a large group of them, waving his hand in jaunty fashion, and then shook hands with a few astonished Frenchmen who were not expecting to see him and therefore could form no clear conception of his identity. In a similar situation I should have felt embarrassed; not so the Field Marshal, who walked quickly and smilingly on to his car and off we drove to Courances.

Courances is a handsome eighteenth-century château set in the usual spacious gardens and parkland. Its most notable feature is an elegantly curved double stone staircase leading from the garden to a first-floor entrance. In the garden are many waterworks of traditional style. On arrival the Field Marshal conducted me about his property explaining just as if he had been a sapper the various water-levels and pointing out particular trees and shrubs. He was interested in a proprietary way and he had many plans for garden parties and cocktail parties worked out in his head to the last detail. He would receive his guests at the top of the stone staircase whence they would debouch into the large reception rooms or back into the garden if the weather was fine. He was evidently tickled with his new position and the rank and privilege which went with it. When a young man he no doubt set his sights high and aimed at the greatest power and influence which the Army can confer; but it can never have entered his young head that he would one day be the proprietor of a French château and the grand seigneur of the neighbouring villages. He intended, quite rightly, to make the most of this chance and to get the greatest possible enjoyment out of it. He always had a zest for life and he always liked the centre of the stage. Here was a different scene and a different part—the great British conqueror turned into a smiling English 'Milor' dispensing favours from a French throne.

The day was hot and I could have done with a slight pause and rest, but no sooner was our tour of the property completed than we set out again. This time we were accompanied by two A.D.C.s, one British and one French, and I think also by George Cole, his military assistant at this time. We proceeded on foot through the dusty streets of two neighbouring villages, of which he was, or deemed himself to be, by virtue of his residence at the château, the grand seigneur. We passed the time of day with the somewhat astonished villagers as we went along and we entered various small shops and estaminets and some private cottages. At each port of call the Field Marshal, whose command of French at this time was little more than the rusty recollection of his lessons at St. Paul's, would call out, in high good humour and without the least trace of self-consciousness, a series of direct questions—'*Ah! madame, comment allez-vous? Combien d'enfants avez vous?*' Or to the men: '*Êtes-vous soldat? Moi je suis soldat. Beaucoup de médailles? Bon. Vous-êtes blessé?*

Ah! dans la grand guerre.' In some places which we visited our reception, I thought, was less than warm. In the first place nobody was expecting to see the Field Marshal and it took them a little time to realise who he was. In the second place it never became clear to most of them why he had come to see them. He bought nothing from them and I suspect they would have welcomed him more warmly if they had seen the colour of his money. In other places, however, notably where there was an elderly man who had fought in the first world war, the effect was touching. After a minute's uncertainty the old peasant would grasp the Field Marshal's hand and with tears in his eyes insist on showing him his medals and relics of war.

We must have spent two hours, I should think, on this strange excursion. I was hot and tired on return to the château and glad to be told that dinner would not be before 8 p.m. That gave me two hours for a rest and a bath. I calculated, wrongly as it happened, that there would be no drinks before dinner and that it would be better to stay in my room until eight o'clock. I descended a minute or two before eight and was immediately offered a cocktail or a glass of sherry. I swallowed quickly, so as not to offend the Field Marshal's sense of punctuality, and we went into dinner—an entirely masculine affair composed of the same officers who had made the patronage tour. In traditional style M. le Curé had been asked to join us, but he had found some reasons for excusing himself. The Field Marshal was most hospitable and, contrary to my expectation, wine was served freely. The course of the conversation has been long forgotten. The main topic was, I think, corporal punishment—something which we had probably all suffered at some stage or other and about which the young men could be expected to have views. It was not conversation in the ordinary sense; there was no spontaneous exchange of remarks, no flow from one topic to another. The topics were set pieces. The Field Marshal would set out the topic in provocative fashion and then call upon each in turn to make his comment. 'Now I would say,' he would begin, 'that corporal punishment is a very good thing and that everybody is the better for a good beating. Now what would you say?' And having thrown this opinion into the midst he would intervene from time to time with teasing questions—'Were you ever beaten at school? What was it for? Why didn't they beat you more often? Don't you think you would have been more lively and alert if you had been?' and so on. When that topic seemed to have been exhausted another would be introduced in the same style— jocular, provocative and intellectually superficial. Serious political matters and the problems of the moment were avoided. This was leisure time and the boys were present. It was rather like dinner with the benevolent and facetious housemaster. It was so designed, it was deliberate. This was the time of day for a little joking and the joking must be geared to the youngest member of the party. The youngest member of the party probably thought that his level was misjudged, but at least the conversation did not die away into a nervous silence.

The form after dinner was still informal but less convivial. The Field Marshal was about to give a large cocktail party and he wanted to go through the list of guests. This was produced and we all stood round a table discussing the correctness of the list, the claims of those on it and of those omitted from it. When this had been exhaustively completed the arrangements were discussed, the drill for the reception and dispersal of the guests, the type of food and drink to be served, etc. Throughout this we remained standing and unrefreshed. Abruptly at about 10.30 the Field Marshal said good night and went to his room. With a sort of furtive shame I sank into a chair and begged the A.D.C. for a nightcap. It had been a long day.

Dinner With de Lattre

It would be a grievous misuse of language to say that relations between the Field Marshal and General de Lattre were not very cordial. In fact their mutual animosity over a considerable period was venomous. I believe that before General de Lattre left for his fateful task in Indo-China there had been, thanks to Field Marshal Slim, a reconciliation, but I doubt very much if the personal wounds inflicted by the one upon the other in these early unhappy days would ever have been permanently healed. Fundamentally they were both vain men. They were both strong and dominating personalities. They were both accomplished professionals, although, of course, the Field Marshal's military renown was far more widely acknowledged. They both loved power and they were both supremely self-confident in the exercise of it. When men share these particular attributes it is hard for them to work in harness. Each had his full share of national pride, but it was not this which caused the disharmony. Had they both been English or both French it would have been just the same. In fact both were devoted to the cause of West European unity for which we all worked. The Field Marshal was well ahead of British military opinion in his pursuit of this object and he did lay himself out to understand French problems and to acquaint himself with French ways and with the French language. General de Lattre was really of much the same mind. He liked the British. He was amused by us and he sometimes mocked us with subtle ironic humour, but he liked us. He took pride in his Scottish ancestry. If I remember rightly, his great-grandfather had gone into exile with Charles X and had married a Scottish lady. When I first knew him he spoke little English, though he understood it well enough. When I last saw him he could speak well if he had a mind to. Their respective manners

174

and style could not have been more different. The Field Marshal terse and trenchant, given to oversimplification, ignoring or despising tangential considerations, using straight-forward language unadorned except by idiom borrowed from the world of sport, jocular with a kind of puerile humour, practical, decisive, self-assured, uneasy in the realm of specula-tive ideas, unacquainted with art and literature, undemonstra-tive, though not without affection for lesser beings, flinty and unyielding, careless of personal feelings, insensitive to them, single-minded, somewhat ascetic, precise and punctual. General de Lattre, delighting in words and figures, leaving the highway of his talk for intriguing by-paths, elaborating and refining his expressions, dwelling in irony and wit, amused with life and with people, alternating wildly between anger and compassion, rage giving place to tears, acting somewhat, enthusiastic for life and art, loving people, including those whom he most violently chastened, tender and sensitive and yet in many ways unpardon-ably inconsiderate and unreasonable, taking pleasure in the flesh-pots, good wine, good company, good talk, uncontrolled and hopelessly unpunctual.

In my position I had not expected that I should have any direct personal contact with General de Lattre. The usual channel of communication between the Commanders-in-Chief Committee and the Western Union Chiefs of Staff Committee and the Ministers of Defence was Major-General Belchem, the Field Marshal's Chief of Staff; to me and vice versa. This was quite normal and acceptable, except that we both happened to be British. Moreover, General Belchem, though he had many French friends and spoke French well, if in a somewhat florid and quite un-English way, was not liked or trusted by General de Lattre. General de Lattre was inclined to attribute the Field Marshal's animosity to the influence of General Belchem. Whether justified or not, that was his feeling, and it was a short step from that to include me in the orbit of

his suspicion and mistrust. When decisions of Ministers of
Defence seemed to him to favour the Field Marshal's point of
view, rather than his own, he began to scent a sort of con-
spiracy in which I was in deep and secret league with the Field
Marshal and General Belchem and was being used by them as a
useful agent when matters came to the level of the Western
Union Chiefs of Staff and the Ministers of Defence. I never
should have been aware of this had it not been for the loyalty
of the French officers on my staff, more particularly Colonel de
Rougemont. They had their ears to the ground and they
presently reported to me that General de Lattre's anger was hot
against me and that it was his strongly held opinion that I was
abusing my position and privilege to further the interests of the
Field Marshal against his own. I think I was more angry than
surprised. I had already incurred some odium with my countrymen for seeming to them to be doing precisely the opposite.
Any man in my position has to expect that sort of thing. He
cannot possibly please five countries all the time. I well knew,
for example, that Colonel Cumont, the highly gifted Belgian
officer who in effect ran the Belgian delegation, regarded me
as cunning and unscrupulous—'*ce malin Mallaby*' he called me.
But he was quite prepared to come and say it to me himself.
What angered me was that General de Lattre should be talking
in opprobrious and damaging terms about me behind my back
and seeking to undermine the friendship and confidence which
I had earned from the French. I was angry, too, because there
was no truth whatever in the accusations he was levelling
against me.

I accordingly asked Colonel de Rougemont to let General de
Lattre know that I had heard some disquieting rumours and to
request him to send someone to me to explain in person the
errors and crimes of which he held me to be guilty. He acceded
to this request, saying to de Rougemont at the same time: '*Je ne
dis pas que Mallaby est un homme de Montgomery. En effet je ne*

*trouve pas qu'il aime Montgomery particulièrement, mais comme
même il est britannique et il manie les affaires d'une façon avantageuse
à ses compatriotes.'* This notion of being *un homme de* someone or
other is, or was, prevalent in the French Army. A prominent
senior officer would become attached to junior officers serving
on his staff and would tend to keep them in his entourage,
embracing their careers with his, advancing or retarding them
according to his own success or failure. This system permits
touching manifestations of personal devotion and loyalty, but it
is open to serious objection. It encourages personal patronage
and favouritism and it creates division and disunity in the Army
as a whole. It was feared at one time that the glorious ascent of
Field Marshal Montgomery during the war was bringing the
same system into favour with us. There would be no rewards,
no high positions, for officers who had not served in the
8th Army, it was alleged, but I doubt if there is much
evidence that he ever worked a system of patronage. He was
himself fully aware of the unity and force which the unquestioned pre-eminence of the C.I.G.S. gave to the British
Army and he used to enquire from Frenchmen, with teasing
provocation, who was the head of their Army. He never
received a satisfactory answer.

Colonel Cogny was deputed by General de Lattre to see me
and explain the reasons for his mistrust. Colonel Cogny was
unmistakably *un homme de* de Lattre and he found it almost
impossible to believe that I was not *un homme de* Montgomery.
In consequence our dinner together was not the happiest of
occasions. He started a vigorous attack upon a position which I
was not occupying and my counter-attack came, therefore, from
an unexpected direction. It was no business of mine to defend
the Field Marshal's conduct of his job or to criticise General de
Lattre for his handling of the land forces. I was concerned only
with the General's attack upon me. In what respects and on
what occasions had I abused the privilege of my international

M

status to advance British interests against French? Accusations
of this kind were irresponsible and undermined the confidence
in the central secretariat, which with the aid of my Five-Power
staff I had succeeded in creating. If there was any solid justification for such charges General de Lattre should report them to
the French Minister of Defence and he could examine them
with his four colleagues. It was to them I was responsible in the
last resort. If the General was unwilling to do this he should
keep silent. There was nothing more damaging and more unfair than the uncontrolled whispering of malice. I grew more
heated than I had intended and perhaps more than I felt.
Colonel Cogny was distressed and rather angry and hastily
switched the direction of his attack, but there was not much
power in his punch. I do not remember how it all ended. I think
that in calmer style we thrashed out a few particular points.
The courtesies of the dinner table were maintained and Colonel
Cogny promised, with some misgiving I thought, to report our
conversation to General de Lattre.

For a few weeks I heard no more. Then I was told that the
General had been partly reassured by what Colonel Cogny had
reported, but that he would like to see me in person. Would I
be so good as to dine with him at Claridge's on his next visit to
London? Of course. I could not refuse and only an idiot or a
coward would miss the opportunity of dining with this remarkable man. I confess that I entered Claridge's on 7th December
1949 with a good deal of trepidation. I knew that the General
had a formidable armoury of offence and in position and
prestige I was not in the same street at all. Nor had I in the least
expected that it was to be a single combat. On arrival I was
shown to the General's private suite. He received me courteously. There were perhaps three or four French officers with
him and together we drank an aperitif and exchanged the usual
banalities. We would descend, I supposed, to the dining-room
and after dinner the General and I would talk for half an hour

or so and then rejoin the others—a wholly erroneous supposi-
tion. After about twenty minutes the other officers were
summarily dismissed and I was left alone with the great man.
A waiter was summoned. An excellent, carefully chosen dinner
was ordered, just for the two of us, here in this room. The
waiter withdrew. The assault began. It was sharp rather than
rough, delivered at considerable speed in French, the voice
rising occasionally to a rather shriller note of outrage, and the
mouth closing upon the words in the pout of an insulted man.
There were gestures to match, from time to time a sharp rap
upon the table accompanying a hostile glare, and then a
silencing gesture with the hand to make clear that no interjection from me would be tolerated. The recital of my disloyalties
and perfidious dealings seemed to stimulate the General's face
and figure into curious attitudes. At one moment he looked
like a ruffled bird with feathers awry, at the next like an
emperor giving orders to a slave. It was a splendid performance,
which I would have enjoyed a good deal more if I had been a
spectator and not the object of the attack. I had to listen carefully and keep my head and my temper. Some of the accusations enraged me, malicious gossip picked up from foolish men,
others needed careful analysis and a reasoned answer. It is not
so easy to show anger and resentment in a foreign tongue, but
when the flow ceased, and I was permitted to speak, I made, I
think, a fair attempt. Perhaps in the paucity of my vocabulary
I overdid the word '*injuste*' but in the context it was not a bad
word. At least it was clear that I was hot and bold and that was
really all the General wanted to see. If I had cringed I should
have been written off, but, as it was, as I stammered out my
angry remonstrances, the General's demeanour changed. The
temperature dropped and we discussed in calmness and reason
the few points that deserved this treatment.

The waiters reappeared, the excellent dinner was served, the
General was all smiles and affability and I grew easy and

mellow with the wine. Out of our coldness and resentment, a
friendship began to grow. He talked of everything, of ancestry
and families, of art and literature, of war-time experiences, of
great French and British personalities. He talked, of course,
more than I did. I was very content that it should be so. His
experience of life was longer and much more exciting than
mine and he talked with style and with humour. I was fascinated, almost enchanted, but, with the crude independence of
my Puritan forbears, I had no intention of surrendering to his
charm any more than I had to his rage. For that matter he had
no intention of trying to make me. He had accepted me as a
man of independent spirit. He truly wanted my friendship—I
had no benefits to offer him—and at that strange dinner party I
freely gave it. The hours went by, the dinner was cleared away,
an A.D.C. put his head in at the door and was promptly shot
out. I made tentative efforts to go, but not until 2.30 a.m.
would he agree. At that late hour he accompanied me to the
front door of the hotel and bade me an affectionate good night.
I walked home in the pouring rain, my heart much relieved and
my imagination much stimulated.

I saw him from time to time thereafter—as often, indeed, as
our respective duties and preoccupations permitted. At my
request he accepted an invitation to attend Gaudy Day at
Radley. He loved it and everybody loved him. It was a beautiful sunny day and Radley looked its best. He was the great man,
receiving with gracious smiles and gestures the applause and
admiration of the crowd—a part he played to perfection. He
made a witty and entertaining speech in the open air, standing
with his back to the fine Queen Anne house. He spoke in
French with great clarity, so that everybody could understand
a great deal of what he said. From time to time he interlarded
some English phrases, deliberately enunciated like the prover-
bial Frenchman, and he delighted in the laughter this provoked.
He stayed a night with the Warden, where I fear his obtrusive

and demanding habits caused confusion and inconvenience. Soon after midnight he demanded to see me, but I was fast asleep in a different house and had taken the precaution of making myself incommunicado. If he wanted bananas at 2 a.m. he saw no reason why he should not ring the bell. I fancy that the Warden and Mrs. Wilkes were a little relieved when they saw his car departing to Abingdon. He had enjoyed his visit very much. He often spoke of it, though never without a pained reference to the fact that I had not answered his midnight summons. He liked to discuss public schools, to compare the atmosphere and attributes of those which he had visited and to contrast the system of education in France. '*Je m'interesse beaucoup dans la jeunesse*,' he would say, and the experiment of the Camps Légers is practical evidence that this was no insincerity.

My last official encounter with him was at an exercise which the Field Marshal held at Fontainebleau. The exercise was organised and mounted by the Field Marshal's own staff and was most inappropriately named 'Unity', for at this moment relations between him and General de Lattre could not have been more frigid and unfriendly. The Commanders-in-Chief and all their staffs attended this exercise, together with representatives of Western Union Chiefs of Staff and some of my own central secretariat. The exercise, which lasted two or three days, I think, was opened by the Field Marshal with his customary succinct and confident *exposé*. At the end of this he was prompted by General Belchem to ask if the Commander-in-Chief would like to make any comments or ask any questions. I could see that he did not much relish this. It was his exercise and he wanted to get on with it, but he accepted the advice as a necessary courtesy. Whereupon he turned towards General de Lattre, who was sitting in the front row, and said in his most perfunctory and graceless manner, 'De Lattre, do you want to say anything?' I was truly not surprised that the General

should resent this incivility, offered in the presence of perhaps
200 staff officers; and his uncompromising refusal to say anything but, 'No, I will wait to the end,' spitting out his words
with contempt and dislike, was all that could have been
expected. The failure of the exercise was assured and the irony
of its title gloomily emphasised. Not even a most tactful and
ingenious summary by Field Marshal Slim could save it.

During the course of the exercise it was the custom to adjourn
for lunch to a large building or marquee, I forget which, where
Field Marshal Montgomery and each of the Commanders-in-
Chief had his own table for himself and his own staff. Those of us
who were guests were invited in turn to these tables. On the first
day I was invited to the Field Marshal's table, was received as
always with courtesy and placed in a position quite appropriate
to my status—somewhere, that is to say, amongst the Major-
Generals and Brigadiers. On the second day I was invited to
General de Lattre's table. I was in fact staying with Brigadier
R. H. Barry, who was the General's British Chief of Staff, an
old friend of mine, and I knew that I owed this attention to his
kindness. But on my approach to the table General de Lattre
rose from his seat, pressed forward to greet me warmly, dis-
placed some very important person, and obliged me to sit down
beside him. What was the motive? I have no doubt that he had
noticed, or been told, my comparatively unelevated position
at the Field Marshal's table. Was he still expecting that by this
elaborate display he would enlist my support, such as it was,
against the Field Marshal? Certainly not. I prefer to think—and
I do think—that this was spontaneous friendliness, a certain
feeling of kinship with me. He knew that I was likely to be
cherishing the same thoughts about the exercise as he was. He
knew that in a sometimes hostile world I liked him.

That was my last official encounter with him. Soon afterwards we both left the organisation. I returned to duty as a
British civil servant in the Cabinet Office and he went off to

Indo-China as High Commissioner and Commander-in-Chief
—a testing job which he carried out with immense verve.
Nobody could have established and fortified a permanent
position for France at this stage in that troubled area, but he
made sure at any rate, as nobody else could have done, that the
influence and power of France were not ignominiously
whittled away but went out in a final blaze of glory.

I saw him once more. He was on leave from Indo-China and
paid a visit to London. General Maurice Durosoy, the French
military attaché in London, gentle and popular amongst us,
arranged a small dinner party in his house and was good enough
to ask me. Amongst the guests was General Sir Richard Gale,
the tough Commander-in-Chief B.A.O.R. and later Deputy
Supreme Commander in N.A.T.O. He was a friend and
admirer of General de Lattre, whose conversation held him in
a kind of mesmerised spell. General de Lattre was looking
worn and thin and old. No doubt the illness which killed him
had started to assail him. But his conversation was as lively and
vigorous as ever and there in the presence of men who were
attached to him his personality was mellow and expansive. I
seem to remember that he talked for a good deal of the time in
English, of which by then he had a quite fluent and easy
command. He had, of course, had many contacts with the
British Service and political chiefs in Malaya who were engaged
in an uphill and obstinate struggle against the terrorists. It was
in the days before the supreme civil and military powers were
united in the hands of Sir Gerald Templer and the General in
his best ironic vein described the British system of conducting
the war. It was an elaborate and ingenious network of committees, he said. Any one committee which succeeded in
coming to a decision was obliged to refer that decision to
another committee, whose duty it was, so it often seemed, to
reverse it or annul it or at best to refer it to yet another committee. By this means nobody became too powerful, no envies

or jealousies were generated, but the terrorists remained undisturbed. The criticism was lively and light-hearted, not
intended to wound, but it was by no means misplaced, as
subsequent events showed. General Gale sat spellbound and
entranced by this display of irony and wit and from time to
time punctuated the glittering monologue with a violent
beating of his thigh and loud cries of 'By God! he's right, you
know. By God! he's right.'

That was a happy evening, but I went home sad at heart. I
could not help feeling that I should never see this brilliant
creature again. In a few months he was dead.

The Council of
Foreign Ministers

Although the defence organisation worked as a separate self-
contained unit headed by the five Ministers of Defence they
themselves were responsible to the Council of Five Foreign
Ministers who were the top layer of the Treaty. These five
Foreign Ministers had permanent representatives on a committee in London with a Secretariat-General presided over by
M. Star-Busmann, a Dutch diplomat. My contacts with him
were naturally close and frequent. When meetings of the five
Foreign Ministers themselves took place, on the same rotatory
and peripatetic principle as the Ministers of Defence, I attended
them, along with M. Star-Busmann and his staff, to speak for
the defence organisation and give an account of its progress.
These occasions were a delight to me. The main burden of the
work was not on my shoulders. I had time and leisure to look

about me and enjoy myself—at any rate after my ordeal was over. It could be an ordeal—to defend our plans and dispositions before politicians whose temperaments seem to incline them to mistrust and despise military men and before diplomats some of whom find it much easier to sneer than to cheer. I did not always escape unscathed from the harsh misgivings of M. Spaak and the contempt of Gladwyn Jebb. I was by no means the only man to suffer in this respect. But I confess I was not really much hurt by these in the face of the warm encouragement I always received from M. Bech and M. Robert Schuman and Ernest Bevin.

One of the early meetings of this Council of Ministers took place at The Hague. I travelled by sea from Harwich to the Hook to attend it. Anxious as always—perhaps absurdly so—to retain and emphasise my objective international status, I was careful to keep myself somewhat aloof from the United Kingdom delegation and Ernie Bevin who were travelling by the same route. It was a Sunday and the train was behind time reaching Harwich and the boat set out for the Hook two hours late. It was a pleasant fine day and a calm sea. At sea the sense of urgency drops away. If you are late you are late and there is nothing you can do about it. This easy and relaxed sensation brought relief and comfort to Ernie Bevin, overstrained, overworked. He sent for me to join him in the bar. It was the first occasion, I think, on which I had had any close personal contact with him. He was easy and friendly and warm. There was something about me which he liked and from that day until his death he never wavered in his friendship and kindness to me. We exchanged jokes and stories. We had a drink or two. We laughed and were at ease, with some hours of calm sea ahead of us and nothing urgent to do. These indolent feelings were soon shattered. Suddenly on rapid little feet came bustling in the assiduous, efficient, dutiful private secretary rubbing delighted hands and announcing in smug, unctuous

tones: 'It's quite all right, Secretary of State, I've seen the
Captain and he is going to make up lost time. We shall get to
the Hook on the hour.' 'What the bloody 'ell did you do that
for?' was Uncle Ernie's immediate debunking response. The
poor private secretary perhaps felt very deflated. He did not
look it—and, anyway, of course he was right. British Foreign
Secretaries cannot be late. Too much has been arranged. Too
many people are involved. But Uncle Ernie's rough-and-ready
come-back was characteristic—dislike of officialdom and the
complacent domineering ways of official advisers, delight at an
unexpected escape from his own problems and his own importance and spontaneous anger at its sudden termination,
expressed in his customary unvarnished vernacular. He was all
smiles at once and the poor deflated one was brought into the
circle and given a drink. I have seen Uncle Ernie more than
once irritated to the limits of his patience by the attentive
anxiety of his Foreign Office advisers. They would crowd
round him at Conferences, by his side and behind his back,
pushing their written advice under his nose, whispering in his
ear. He would brush them all aside with a wave of his large
ungainly hand exclaiming: 'Leave me alone, can't you? I'm not
a bloody baby.' But they loved him. They loved him all the
same and their importunate advice and solicitude were a
measure of their love.

In the course of this particular Conference at The Hague the
French Government fell and poor M. Bidault found himself
démissioné. It made no difference. There was nothing unusual
about it in those days. M. Bidault put up with the chaff of his
colleagues and carried on as usual. The only open controversy
on this occasion, so far as I can remember, was the meaning of
the French word '*notamment*', which had been used in the
communiqué. There was always trouble about these things and
it entertained me to see M. Bidault's trim feathers much
ruffled because a Dutchman presumed to know more about the

French language than he did. This was the kind of argument
from which Uncle Ernie willingly withdrew his attention and
he was glad enough to carry me off to the Embassy garden.
There we sat *tête-à-tête* with a whisky and soda in our hands
enjoying our talk and our laughter until he was dragged away
to address the Embassy staff.

Twice, I think, these meetings took place in Luxembourg—
one of them being a joint meeting of Foreign and Defence
Ministers. Twice I attended an evening reception at the court
of the Grand Duchess—charming anachronism. It might have
been a small German principality in the middle of the eigh-
teenth century—functionaries in powdered wigs, knee-
breeches, silk stockings, gorgeous coats, carrying wands of
office and strutting through the resplendent rooms like haughty
turkey cocks—champagne in long fluted glasses—and all the
protocol of a court. Before the entrance of the Grand Duchess
and her consort, Prince Felix, we were all lined up and then
presented in turn. The royalty then retired to their own
apartment and gave audience to two or three of us at a time
throughout the evening. M. Star-Busmann and I and a M. de
Baerdemacker, a charming young Belgian, on his staff, were
received at the same time. M. Star-Busmann was seated upon
the sofa in close converse with the Grand Duchess, while M. de
Baerdemacker and I chatted with Prince Felix in another part
of the room. Our conversation, which was conducted partly in
French and partly in English, turned for the most part upon the
shooting and eating of game birds. The savour of grouse was
compared with that of partridge, the laws governing '*la chasse*'
in Luxembourg were explained and then M. de Baerdemacker,
who was young and shy and silent, was asked about the game
laws in Belgium. This direct question from so august a person-
age stunned him. He sat absolutely mute. He may have known
nothing about the subject, but whether he did or not his lips
refused to frame any sort of a reply. After an uneasy silence I

made so bold as to press the savoury claims of snipe upon Prince
Felix and the audience ended in great good humour.

At one of these Conferences in Paris an incident remains clear
and remarkable in my memory. We were meeting at the Quai
d'Orsay and it was ordained that there should be a restricted
session—a session confined to the Foreign Ministers themselves
with only one or two advisers each, a very small section of the
secretariat and no interpreters. Because the discussion was
likely to have an important bearing on defence and on the plans
to be made by the Chiefs of Staff and Commanders-in-Chief, I
was admitted to this session. Each Foreign Minister gave his
view in turn. M. Schuman spoke at length in French with a
strong German accent. In the course of this Uncle Ernie, who
could not understand a word, beguiled the time by cleaning his
fingernails with a pen which he found on the tray in front of
him, his large hands sprawled upon the table, no attempt made
to conceal this uninhibited and rather necessary operation.
Nobody was offended. Uncle Ernie could do what he liked.
When M. Schuman had finished he was translated by M.
Roland de Margerie—one of his chief advisers. M. de Margerie
is bilingual, or very nearly so, and his rendering was excellent,
far better than any official interpreter could do. But better still
was to come. Uncle Ernie, of course, listened most carefully to
the translation and then began a rambling discourse in English.
At any rate the words used were English, but as often happened
in his extempore utterances syntax and grammar were wanting.
Moreover, the thought was imprecise, the logic of the argument not easy to discern and the language not always appropriate to the thought. Nevertheless, to those of us who had listened
to these oracular musings before, it was quite clear that some
big idea was slowly mustering in that great head and when he
came to the end of his speech we knew what it was, but we
were perplexed and worried about making the French understand anything at all about it. We need not have worried. With

hardly a moment's pause M. de Margerie began the interpretation into French and in clear, distinct, well-marked, well-
expressed phrases reproduced the full force and flavour of Mr.
Bevin's idea. It was a most remarkable *tour de force*.

I was to see more of Mr. Bevin in the few years that followed
—years in which his powers declined, though not his prestige,
years of painful physical struggle ending in his death. I am very
glad to recall these glimpses of him at Brussels Treaty Conferences, when his fame was high, his capacity for ideas undiminished and his negotiating powers strong and forceful. He was
the great man of Europe in these days, widely acknowledged
and much loved.

There has been no chronological design about these reflec-
tions and although this glimpse of Ernie Bevin is by no means
the latest in time, it is the last of the unwritten minutes which
in this book I want to pull out of the recesses of my memory.
Great political leaders, great Service chiefs, men 'conspicuous
in the nation's eye', have walked in and out of my pages. Over
the space of fifteen years or so I observed them in silence and
for the most part in admiration, if sometimes enlivened by
critical judgment and a touch of light-hearted mockery. All my
chief actors are men who carried a burden of responsibility
which would have crushed and obliterated the average man.
They never shirked this burden and they never used their power
for selfish ends. They loved power, of course; Aristotle pointed
out long ago that that is a distinguishing feature of Man. But
they exercised it invariably for what they judged to be the
country's good. The results of their policies and of their
decisions are now plain for all to see and to argue and fight
over. Should we have shelled the French fleet in 1940? Should
we have sought to defend Greece and Crete? Was General
Eisenhower right about the strategy in north-western Europe?
Did we give India independence too soon? Should South
Africa have left the Commonwealth? There is no end of

questions to tease the amateur statesmen and strategists as they sit around in their clubs and linger over their port. The great debate goes on. Not even in forty or fifty years' time, when historians and publicists will be free to drown themselves in documents, will there be an unquestioned school solution to all these controversies. I only hope that those who are too prone to form harsh judgments will be reminded, by reading this book, that the men who made the decisions were human beings, sometimes tenacious, sometimes frail, leaning one day to severity and to compassion the next, anger and impatience giving place to an irresistible inclination to laughter, pomp and vanity swallowed up by courage and concentration—except in degree not unlike me and you, my patient reader.

Epilogue

THE excitement and hope, the faith and self-confidence, of the young man in delighted pursuit of the vision splendid give place by imperceptible degrees to the stagnant assumptions of middle life, the certainty that experience is the key to truth, experience, that is, allied with a continuing vitality of mind and body. The middle-aged alone can see the way and control the pace. The young are eager, rash and callow. The elderly are feeble, timid and uncertain. They have experience, it is true, but experience allied with failing powers of mind and body. But in fact what the elderly have lost is not so much their powers of mind and body as the arrogance of middle age, and its longing for fame and power and praise. That fevered contest is over. For them, Coleridge's own epitaph:

Mercy, for praise; to be forgiven, for fame,
He asked and hoped through Christ. Do thou the same.

The retired man has leave at last to step off the field of contest and watch from the side-lines, watch the continuing fury of the competition. Yet what interests him more, perhaps, is the watch he has time to keep over his own life, over his own heart.

To Wordsworth it seemed in his old age that his life had been largely wasted. What, then, can be the backward, desperate, hopeless regrets of the common man? And yet inside me, as I come to the end of what will seem to some severe minds trivial recollections of the high and mighty, the most persistent question is not how much better I might have done (though that is certainly true) but who am I? Who is this man who through ten or fifteen busy years received these impressions? In light-hearted fashion and without malice I have performed a superficial vivisection of my actors. It is much harder to do the same operation on myself—and to my readers it could be of little interest or entertainment. But from my level there is something more to be done, an act of piety to be performed, and any reader who has enjoyed these pages will indulge me if in this epilogue I pay a tribute to a few men, far less renowned than all these Prime Ministers and war-time leaders, but men whose influences are so strong in me that I see and understand as they taught me to see and understand. Theirs are influences that I can identify far more readily than I can the influences of my forbears, for the most part imperfectly remembered or not remembered at all. Their influence no doubt I cannot escape, but except in the private recesses of my own family I cannot identify or define it. My brother and I never had any doubt about the source of our strength. We had different talents, different ambitions and different sensibilities—but different as they were they had a common strength which was derived from the powerful and courageous and sensitive personality of my mother, who met extreme adversity with extreme fortitude; who never, in the most arduous and miserable years of absolute penury, surrendered her high standards, never lost her style and quality. We were brought up in poverty, the result of the rash generosities of my father and his somewhat wayward attachment to any form of steady work. He was feckless and unstable, but lovable, charming and tender-hearted, and although he brought my mother, once comparatively affluent and well-to-do, to complete poverty I never heard her say a bitter word against him. To my brother and me he was not much more than a rather sad and perplexing memory. My sister, who is older, has clearer and happier memories of him. His last years were broken by debilities of mind and body and he died when we were very young. No doubt by the laws of heredity some parts of him lived on in us. I cannot precisely measure what these parts were, but from time to time during our boyhood my mother would say to one or other of us, 'You have a great look of your father today,' or 'That is just the sort of joke your father would have made'. From these chance remarks and from her conversation and anecdotes about him I know the sort of man he was, and indeed in the inner workings of my mind and heart I feel at times as I know he would have felt, I react to situations as he would have reacted. He had, I know, some ingenuity of mind, an inventive talent and some facility with words; he was struck and amused by incongruities of expression, by double meanings, and he took great delight in rhyming. He loved nonsense and silliness of all kinds. A long road of individual jokes and laughter led through his life. On his first visit to my mother's family—proud, reserved, conventional—he had invented some foolish game which entailed shouting out 'Rot' —as one might say 'Snap' or 'Beaver'. Coming down to break-fast on his first morning in that austere household, he gaily pushed open the drawing-room door and called out 'Rot', only to find the whole family and all the servants on their knees for family prayers. At the end of the road, when all was weakness and poverty, he was still ready with a jest. The widow of some friend who had committed suicide, knowing our circum-stances, sent my father a suit of his clothes. When it arrived the trousers were missing. 'I suppose,' said my father, 'that he shot himself through the trousers.'

In so far as he ever had a profession he was an actor and if he

N

could have persevered he would have been comfortably in the ranks of those 'safe' actors who are the pillars of the English stage. But he could not persevere. He was too convivial, too easy-going, eager to cut a dash and make a show without any of the hard work needed to give it sense and substance. He was gay and good-looking, he had expensive tastes, in clothes, in cigars, in wines, if he had a sovereign he spent twenty-five shillings, he gambled rashly, he wanted the world to think him a very fine gentleman, and so he was and so for a time the world thought him. But creditors will not wait for long, they grow inquisitive and want to see the colour of your money; and when all my mother's fortune had been spent there was nothing left to show.

My mother's background and training had not in the least equipped her to deal with a situation of this kind. Her family was well connected, exclusive, fastidious. Until her marriage she had been carefully protected and elegantly brought up, and the restrictions of this narrow conventional life were, in fact, an affront to her free spirit. She had had no contact whatsoever with the world of the theatre, with race-meetings, with poker-players, with raffish Bohemian characters—still less with creditors and debts and bailiffs. The early years of married life opened her eyes to unimagined worlds, to what must have seemed to her extravagant personalities and careless living. But she loved life. It was a rich experience to be relished and enjoyed. In her married life she was always ready to meet the demands made upon her. When my father could no longer afford to pay the salary of a leading lady in a play he had put on at the old Strand Theatre my mother stepped into the breach and played the part herself. She played it very well and throughout her life she contributed the professional touch to many an amateur show. When my father thought in his sanguine way that there was money to be made in South Africa she entered upon the adventure with spirit and when it all ended in failure she endured it with the same spirit. How she managed to sustain this lively spirit and this fresh courage as the years brought increasing anxieties and fears, debts and rows and miseries, I do not know. She had pride and self-respect of a conspicuous order. The world was not to see her whine and cringe over what she regarded as her failure to give her husband strength. At all times and in all circumstances she continued to comport herself with poise and dignity. She could never now afford good clothes but she continued to look as if she could.

When the crash came and there was nothing left (nothing, that is, beyond £5 a week) we lived in the simplest possible way in a tiny flat in an obscure part of London; there were no luxuries of any kind and every penny counted. We all helped, we learnt housework and cooking and shopping and we were very happy. We were very happy because my mother faced this situation not only with courage but with gaiety and laughter and resource. We made our own pleasures, we invented our own jokes, we were free and independent, we laughed and we loved each other. She never let us imagine for a moment that our poverty and our lowliness in any way degraded us. Outward circumstances were nothing. Our strength and our happiness were within and by our brave conduct, our high endeavours, our sense of humour and our energy of living, we could overcome our circumstances. She was my life's star. These were her finest years and to her example and her love as I advanced from eight to eighteen—the age 'when men are growing out of boys'—I attribute my fundamental strength— and so, without any question, would my brother.

He was two years older than I, always took the lead in all our games and other pursuits. He was blessed with good brains and good looks and we shared a sense of humour, deep, compelling and inexhaustible. He was a king of nonsense and to this day I can laugh outright and uncontrolled at much of our boyhood's silliness. He grew to manhood as the first world war approached its end and, almost by force of circumstances, he made his career in the Indian Army. I do not think he ever regretted it. He loved his sepoys and his regimental duties, he passed, effortlessly almost, in and out of the Staff College at Camberley, he filled one staff job after another with increasing distinction. With this rapid ascent of the military ladder went a most striking development and expansion of his natural qualities. A sense of panache in the early years of manhood gave place by steady degrees to an outstanding devotion to his duty and to his own family. More than any man I ever knew he went from strength to strength, 'from well to better daily self-surpassed', never stagnant or complacent, never resting on his laurels. In the foothills of fame he met an untimely death at the hand of an Indonesian assassin, leaving behind him a fair name, a fine family and countless admirers, and with me an inheritance of perseverance, calm judgment, laughter and divine nonsense.

Schoolmasters, too, can exert powerful influence, more powerful with sensitive boys than they always like to realize. Acts of retribution, words of sarcastic malevolence, sneers of impatience, easy jesting which sacrifices the feelings of one to the laughter of many—these are remembered, sometimes with pain and resentment through a lifetime. It is wiser and happier to remember the thorough and liberal cultivation with which good schoolmasters tend their young plants—rough sometimes, even angry, but directed towards the aim of a full and satisfying growth.

Over my early years a large dark Kitchener-like figure reigned in alternating moods of encouraging solicitude and ferocious anger. The smiles that played about his dark eyes and lurked shyly behind his heavy black moustache turned quickly and often to the flash of lightning and the clap of thunder. I was afraid of him but I wanted to please him, not only through fear of his vindictive anger but because he seemed to my young heart to be an example of strength and manhood, the sort of person I would have to emulate if I wanted to be a worth-while man myself. It was clear that if I was going to do that I must first master the elements of the Latin language. Foolish blunders in this branch of knowledge seemed to fill him with an over-powering sense of righteous indignation, as if he were person-ally affronted by a falseness of concord or quantity, driven on by gusts of uncontrollable rage at fumbling mistranslations of classical texts. Often have I stood before him striving with childish ignorance and folly to interpret the tirades of Cicero against Catiline and failing lamentably, only to be seized by the button of my jacket, shaken violently to and fro to his im-passioned refrain—'You are as slipshod and slovenly as you can stick together'—and finally slapped sharply across the face and sent back to my seat with the tears falling fast upon the blurred and confused rhetoric of that hateful Roman consul. My fellow sufferers looked on in pity and terror, feeling sure that a similar fate awaited them; and an awed hush fell upon that ancient, inconvenient schoolroom in which two forms of small boys were taught by two schoolmasters where once years before cooks had prepared sumptuous dishes for Archbishop Becket.

But I did learn the elements of the Latin language. I was well grounded, well drilled, well disciplined. My mind became much more effective, more comprehending, an instrument for my own use. I learnt to labour and think to the point, to hang on till I was sure and satisfied. The same sort of lessons in the physical world I learnt on the rugby football field from this same mighty man, who had himself played on the wing for Oxford University. He could keep wicket, too, in first-class company and he was a formidable Captain in the Officers' Training Corps. If one man could do all these things so well, why not another? Over these boyish ambitions inspired in me by this alarming hero the Cathedral presided with a frightening magnificence and the beauty of the music and singing sank deep into my heart.

My hero's name was Algernon Latter, himself educated at the King's School, Canterbury, and Trinity College, Oxford, at this time Headmaster of the Junior King's School, then housed in the middle of Canterbury hard by the Archbishop's Palace. Subsequently he became Headmaster of the King's School itself. In later years I saw him now and again at Twickenham at an international match or at the 'Varsity match and he greeted me always with embracing smiles and a large friendliness. I owe him much.

At Radley my horizons were wider, my freedom in some directions much greater. At my books I could be active or idle more or less as I pleased, or as I dared. From some dons I preferred approbation to abuse. Their tongues could lash and their punishments used up the day. With others it was easy enough to lounge amiably along, neither striving for praise nor fearing rebuke. At games and physical exercises it was more difficult to suit oneself. There were frightening 'bloods'—large rawboned athletic boys—to hound one on, shouting and cursing at any display of wavering fatigue. The prefects seemed only too often intent to detect some trifling misdemeanour in dress or convention hallowed by tradition of which you could not possibly be aware, and to exact the due penalty in corporal punishment, in the imposition of 'lines' or in scathing and tasteless abuse. I feared all this, I must confess, but it kept me alert; and in the sluggish teenage years that is something to be thankful for. In leisure hours, secure from the suspicious eye of authority, there was wide and welcome freedom, freedom to roam in lovely parkland, to visit the river and swim under the Sandford lasher, to watch one's cricket heroes all a summer's afternoon, to sit and talk and laugh and fool about, to make friends, golden friends, and never to question their brilliance and their devotion. Then there were ugly setbacks, friendships which cooled, affection which seemed to turn into indifference or contempt, zeal and enthusiasm which were frowned upon and regarded as common and inappropriate, dons who from heights of wisdom and good taste seemed suddenly to descend to retributive meanness and pettiness, and others, whom it was the fashion to despise, raised in a moment by some single act of skill or kindness to a level of emulation and regard. The dreaded puberty accounted for much trouble and uncertainty. Everything was secret and dark and fearful and those who had mastered it with a confident arrogance were suspect and alarming—and yet had a godlike magnetism about them because they were in control where we were not.

Much of this I remember and indeed feel and know as if it were yesterday, but in the intervening years a process of selection has imperceptibly taken place. The fear and the dread are long since allayed. To be late for early school, to be unclean or idle on parade, to funk at a game, to wilt and fail on a cross-country run, to be caught talking or smiling in chapel, to trespass on ground reserved for the feet of prefects, to be required to construe a passage heedlessly unprepared, to cultivate friendships out of one's class and age group—these dreadful sins and solecisms are forgotten and no longer even haunt one's dreams. What is remembered is good and happy—the friendships which endured, the growing strength of mind and body, the dawn of intellectual interest, the increase of skill and control, the companionship and fun, the groping towards a Christian life— and the men who by precept and example persuaded us to attempt the full exercise of our faculties.

Some of the teaching was brisk, efficient and unimaginative, some pedestrian in the extreme, some patently inadequate, fit only to provoke inattention or derision, and some, but not very much, of distinction and quality. Into the last category of teachers came unquestionably the odd and individual figure of W. R. Smale. He arrived at Radley a term or two before me after a disastrous start to his professional career. Educated at Shrewsbury and New College he was a good classic and a better historian. On going down he went to teach at Clifton where he quite failed to acquire the difficult art of discipline. Wisely he made a move after a year and arrived at Radley determined not to fail twice. In consequence in his first terms his attitude to boys was severe to the point of harshness and even small misdemeanours brought down upon one's head retribution out of all proportion to the offence. As his self-confidence increased his severity diminished and his powers of teaching expanded and developed in a remarkable degree. For the most part, so far as I was concerned, his formal teaching was Latin and Greek— set books, compositions, unseens, at a higher fifth-form level; and subsequently in the classical sixth form, though he was not the form master, he read Virgil with us in school and Homer privately with us in his rooms in the evenings. But my abiding recollection of his teaching is not primarily of his teaching the classics. What started as a period of Latin book might change in the middle to a discussion of Swinburne's poetry and end with a discourse on Church history. His head was stocked with information of all kinds, he reacted quickly to the association of ideas and from him I first learnt the most important point about education—namely that it becomes stimulating and exciting and assumes a real and lasting significance once you realise that knowledge must not be compartmentalised, that the study of Latin grammar, though it must be learned thoroughly and faultlessly, should lead easily and simultaneously to speculations about the type of men who used this language, to examples of the influence of this language upon our own and upon our literature and so on until every day the mind's horizons were pushed further out. I am not sure on looking back that these diffuse and colourful methods were very helpful to my classical scholarship which never came up to my early promise. But they gave me a far greater gift than that; they gave me a delight in knowledge of all kinds for its own sake, they set me off on a love affair with the history and literature of my own country, the flame of which has burned steadily to this day.

Apart from these methods which brought so much richness to my life, I owe a lot to the style and manner in which he operated them. Set on a large body, which can only be described as shapeless and flabby, was a head, a shade too small and with features which justifiably earned him, amongst his colleagues, the nickname of 'Camel'. The protrusion of the lower lip was ugly and as a prelude to some display of wit or some stinging rejoinder he moved it up and down in slow contortions thereby displaying a lot of large yellowish teeth. His eyesight was weak and he affected, in the fashion of the day, rimless pince-nez which above the toothful smile did not add to the physical attractions of his person. He moved awkwardly and on appearance alone he would have seemed in any company strange and eccentric; amongst boys he seemed grotesque. And yet any temptation we might have felt to mock or deride him we very soon suppressed. When he was angry his tongue could lash you cruelly. When he was not angry his conversation was never dull and the large doses of information were illuminated by a pungent wit. I learnt many tricks of speech and phrase from him, just as I learnt to share with him and to retain an intimate admiration for Dr. Johnson, on whom perhaps in some respects he modelled himself. Certainly he knew how to deliver crushing and gratuitous insults. Suddenly in the middle of a period of Greek unseen he turned upon a once highly respected Mayor of Henley-on-Thames: 'Turn your face to the wall, my dear G——T——; you're like a monstrous toad.' Once, when several of us were in his rooms having coffee and buns one Sunday evening, the conversation turned upon performing animals, and one of our number, named Tompkins, in unassuming modesty remarked, 'I once saw a performing bear.' There was a short silence while

Smale's lip moved up and down and then suddenly he shot out, 'I am quite prepared to believe you, my dear Tompkins, but if that is your only title to fame you are likely to remain obscure.'

The unimaginative man-power regulations of the first war removed this brilliant teacher from our midst when we could ill spare him and turned him into a very inefficient and un-soldierly gunner in a home-based regiment of the R.G.A. From this inappropriate occupation he returned for a year or so before I left with a much enriched repertoire of partially true stories about himself. His service to Radley continued until the second world war, when some private and insupportable strain drove him to suicide. He had used up all his reserves of nervous energy.

For the whole of my time in it, the classical sixth form was in the hands of L. A. B. Moss-Blundell, a Wykehamist and a precise and excellent scholar. This sensitive and gifted man did not in fact have the influence with us which his talents and his industry deserved. There was some lack of force in his person-ality, an inability to command our attention or enthusiasm. He would, I think, have been better placed as a don than as a schoolmaster. In those disordered days of the first war school life was short, masters were hard to come by and organization was often makeshift. In consequence many of us arrived in the classical sixth still frivolous and unfledged, not yet spontane-ously devoted to learning. We needed forceful and severe leadership and this Moss-Blundell was not equipped by nature to give. He had, moreover, some mannerisms, some tricks of speech and gesture, which we found a degree grotesque. We seized upon them for daily imitations, which boys so much delight in, and built his whole personality into something strangely freakish and eccentric. We spent more time, more effort, more ingenuity and imagination on this creative non-sense than ever we did on our Greek and Latin compositions. We came to believe in the reality of our strange creation and it was a flat disappointment to me to find, after he had lunched at home with us, that my mother and brother had thought him charming and intelligent, of course, and not in the least an oddity or figure of fun. On looking back now I must confess I was not an apt pupil, not attentive, not sympathetic, more interested in this sensitive and scholarly man as a focus for mockery than as a teacher. I regret it. He had much to teach me and my career would have been easier if I had heeded him. All the same, he has played a considerable part in my life and in the lives of many of my contemporaries. We liked him. He was fundamentally gentle and friendly, though with a strong inclination to sudden impulses of rather futile rage. We picked up from him, in spite of ourselves, something of the scholar's sense of precise discrimination and his harmless idiosyncrasies have regaled us ever since and provide an unbreakable link between those of us who sat together at his ineffectual feet and wasted his time.

For my first three years at Radley, Gordon Selwyn was Warden and for my last two Adam Fox—both of them men of fine quality and individual distinction. Selwyn was a very good scholar, with an outstanding record at Eton and Cambridge. In the classics he was exact and exacting. He expected to see in us at least the beginnings of his own high standards of accuracy and style. It was impossible not to be aware of his own effortless superiority as he sat with a somewhat disdainful air on the dais of the sixth-form classroom. There was a self-assurance about him, even a hint of arrogance, and in spite of his lack of inches a very impressive dignity of bearing. He could be scornful, a little contemptuous if one's response to his questions seemed to him halting or dense. If one was ill-prepared his anger was quiet but tense. I never saw him impatient or rough. His self-control was abundant and he hardly ever raised his voice, but he was never dull. He was less discursive than Smale, sticking more closely to the work in hand and driving one into some

comprehension of detailed points of scholarship. He looked for
accuracy and praised it, but over imaginative or original work
he smiled with delight. I remember well submitting a copy of
Latin verses for a school prize. It was corrected first by Moss-
Blundell, who heavily scored out the false quantities and gross
blunders—I was very young—and awarded it a mark so low
that I was hurt and upset. It was no doubt what it deserved.
The Warden at this point looked through all the copies and
sent for me. The blunders were serious, he pointed out, and Mr.
Moss-Blundell was right to pass a heavy sentence on the copy.
On the other hand, he went on, he had been gratified by one or
two imaginative turns of phrase and if I would take pains to
avoid elementary errors I ought to be able to produce respect-
able, even attractive, Latin verse. How much I loved him for
that and for much else that was broader and deeper, more
human, more sympathetic than mere linguistic excellence on
which all the same he continued to insist. When I was sixteen
he said that I promised to be a really good classical scholar and
I think under his leadership I might have been.

His inspiration as a teacher did not end with the classics. He
was himself a theologian well skilled in the dialectics of this
obscure and difficult subject, but in teaching us he distilled his
own great learning into direct and simple interpretation of the
New Testament. In his sermons, too, he avoided obscurity and
sought to give us straightforward and practical Christian ad-
monishment. But he was not, I think, to schoolboys a particularly successful preacher. He was never a popular figure with
the school as a whole and his manner was too contained, even a
trifle frigid and remote; he had not the histrionic gifts needed
to compel reluctant attention. His teaching of divinity was
formal instruction delivered in chapel on Sunday mornings to
all members of the Upper School, who made full notes as he
went along and could expect trouble if these notes were not
carefully written up and delivered to him by the end of the day.

His informal teaching—as is usually the case—was much more
successful and much more vividly remembered. He exacted
from the members of the sixth a fortnightly or monthly essay
to be done in our own spare time. He was careful to set us
subjects within the compass of our immaturity and he encouraged us to read around the subject and make plentiful use
of illustration and quotation. We took great pains; we were
anxious to please him; and he took as great pains in correcting
and commenting on our efforts and discussing them with us as
he returned them. He would occasionally depart from the strict
regimen of the time-table and devote a whole period to a
discussion of the war situation and an explanation of the
strategy and operations of the time—a subject which he handled
with masterly clarity. In the evenings from time to time he
would invite some of us to his lodgings for poetry-readings and
I have firmly imprinted on my mind a picture of Selwyn sitting
relaxed in an armchair, but still with the slightly arrogant tilt
of his head, reading aloud to us Browning's *Ring and the Book*,
as we sat round that fine drawing-room, enriched by Sewell's
extravagant furniture, in that lovely Queen Anne house.

There was a sinewy strength about Selwyn, a self-confidence
of manner, an unquestioning belief in the moral and intellectual
superiority of those brought up to godliness and good learning
in the traditional discipline of his own great-grandfather, Dr.
Arnold. He never had any doubt, it seemed, that this particular
system of education was right and that a cultivated Englishman,
severely disciplined in this creed, was about as good as you
could get. This deliberate acceptance of standards, very high
standards of excellence in moral and intellectual performance,
marked out a clearly defined path for our footsteps. Although
we often failed and fell in fatigue and frustration by the wayside
we never had any doubt about the right track and the ultimate
destination. I cannot help feeling that pupils of Selwyn,
exclusively apprenticed and devoted to him, might have grown

up, in spite of his liberal and artistic sympathies, in the un-wavering certainty that the Kingdom of Heaven was readily accessible to those educated at Eton and King's and perhaps not much less accessible, if we tried very hard, to the products of Radley and Merton.

If any of us had begun to think like that, the arrival of Adam Fox as Warden in Selwyn's place very soon persuaded us to think otherwise. Fox had been educated in college at Win-chester and at University College, Oxford, and had been for some years a successful assistant master and housemaster at Lancing. He was a good professional schoolmaster and in no sense at all an educationalist. He had no interest in theories of education and indeed he was never quite convinced that the theory, which he was employed to put into practice, was in fact the right one. What was it all about, he kept asking himself, and why in particular did Radley exist, what was its purpose, and what useful contribution did it make to the national life? We all thought ourselves very splendid, we seemed to think it all worth while, and to attach importance to our successes, our prize compositions, our games, our prestige and position; but why were we so sure, was our motive clear, were we severe enough with ourselves, did we really work hard and not just skate elegantly over the surface in well-mannered attitudes? That was enough to disturb our complacency. This quizzical, questioning, doubting, critical approach gave us a salutary shake-up. But it went further. If we were at last convinced that we were doing our best, was it after all worth while doing? What was it all about anyway? 'More things puzzle me', he once wrote on looking at three zebras in a zoo, 'more things puzzle me than puzzle you'—a sentiment which would never have afflicted Selwyn, who did not admit any sensation of puzzlement in himself and who would have thought it a little eccentric to spend time on the contemplation of the mental attitude of zebras. Yet Fox was not really an iconoclast. He was a dreamer, an idealist, and in some respects he looked the part. But there was always another side to him, almost a puritanical streak, a determination, at any rate, to resist an over-indulgence in dreams and affections and to discipline himself to a practical masculine efficiency. His appearance was most striking. He was no taller than Selwyn and had nothing like his dignity of poise and carriage. He was careless about his clothes which often seemed creased and unbrushed. But his head was most impressive. A large arched nose dominated the face and seemed to give to the whole person a determined sense of direction—an impression confirmed by the mouth which was very firm, the lips often setting in a rigid line. The hair was dark, thick, unruly, almost tousled; and under full brows were blue eyes, which changed their brightness with his moods. At times there was a drawn, contemplative look about him, the eyes dimmed to a tone of deep meditation, the mouth set, the head poised and still. At other times the mood was gay, the eyes very bright with an amused gaiety, the mouth flexible with smiling, the tongue ready with sallies of fanciful wit.

But amongst the quicksilver changes of mood his religious faith remained firm and constant. He loved his religion, he loved his Redeemer, with a depth of personal affection, just as he loved his intimate friends. Here there was no wavering at all and he loved in the same manner everything which seemed to him to have its roots in the transcendent love of his religion— great poetry, and especially the poetry of Wordsworth, great thinking, great writing. He was a poet himself, whimsically inclined and not without a touch of mysticism.

I think that perhaps we found him at first a little confusing and did not quite know how to please him, but we loved him very much. He was much warmer and more affectionate than Selwyn, he seemed to like our company and entertained us often and lavishly. Although his classical scholarship was less distinguished than Selwyn's, and he taught us less often, he was exacting in his own way and very severe on loose and careless work. He disliked intensely sprawling sentimentality and he demanded of us masculine habits of thought and style and behaviour. This was, perhaps, to compensate for his inward inclination to detachment and doubt. In all his reports on me, so sensitively imagined and so whimsically phrased, he emphasised over and over again that, for all my gifts in certain directions, I was not very good at getting things done. The lesson went home, since whatever success has come to me has in fact come through my ability to get things done.

It is hard now to disentangle my feelings at the time, when he first came to rule over us forty-five years ago, from my feelings now after a lifetime's friendship. As a boy in authority I was in much more intimate relationship with him than I ever was with Selwyn. He was moreover a much more approachable man. He was young, unmarried, and by nature friendly. He did not much relish the isolated grandeur of his lodgings and the rather remote deference of his staff. He had been accustomed to the easy companionship of the Lancing Common Room and to close and constant contacts with the boys in his house. At Radley he was cut off from all this and he tried to make up for it by encouraging his school prefects to think of themselves as his disciples and friends. It was easy enough for us to do this; and his friendliness to us, not untouched by critical severity if we presumed to relax in it, was the attitude which we in turn tried to adopt towards the rest of the school. In Fox's early years Radley was a very happy place.

I cannot define my debt to Fox. I cannot pin-point it except in one particular. It was he who introduced me to the poetry of Wordsworth, which has been to me ever since a sort of religion. His method of giving advice was strangely inconclusive. He could point out at once the weakness of a proposal, he could estimate the chances of success, he could detect the elements of vanity which lurked in your ambition; but in the end he could never bring himself to come down firmly on one side or the other. Like as not the whole thing seemed to him trivial and unimportant and if a decision had to be made it could be made at the dictates of fancy. He would indeed search for a fanciful reason for deciding a practical issue. I think this lack of precise conviction—except as I insist in matters of religion—was beneficial to those of us who, like me, had felt the unswerving spell of Selwyn. It made us think round and into things before accepting them. It made us wonder whether Radleians were in fact so specially blessed and privileged in the world. It made us question, I think, the whole basis of society and although, so far as I remember, Fox was not remotely interested in Socialism or political radicalism, my thoughts had begun to turn in these directions before I left Radley—partly no doubt because of his own general doubts and misgivings and partly because of the advanced—as it then seemed—political and social thinking of my housemaster in my early years—the Rev. R. H. C. Birt, later Headmaster of the Diocesan College, Rondebosch, Cape Town. In Fox's teaching the most powerful factor was not so much precise scholarship as the exercise of imagination. Nothing should be considered dull and pedestrian if by the exercise of imagination it could be made to come to life. What seemed commonplace became in his handling odd, strange and unusual. His mind and fancy were never stagnant. He was never inactive and he disapproved strongly of 'good-natured lounging' and pointless idleness. To my feelings he gave variety and bright colours, he enlarged my sense of humour and he engaged my affection.

With these models and these standards in my head I began the next stage of my apprenticeship and, in the year 1920, found myself a member of the small and ancient society of Merton College. It was not at all the intention of this epilogue to estimate the worth of the public-school and college systems. Both are now subjected to some strangely misdirected attacks

o

which, for the most part it seems to me, their defenders seek to repel with inappropriate weapons. My intention was to pick out those fine minds and personalities to which from my level I owed acknowledgment. At Merton it is not at all difficult to make the nap selection, but before doing so it is perhaps not out of place, in this mistrusting and uncomprehending generation, to point out what seemed to us, forty and more years ago, the real value of the college system. Between boys and school-masters there must always be some reserve, some barrier of disciplined respect, a certain lack of easy candour and relaxed manners. Between dons and undergraduates this need not be so and in the Merton of 1920 it certainly was not so. We were a lucky generation. The war was just over and in the under-graduate population there was a good percentage of returned warriors, who made my callow mind early acquainted with the realities, both grim and gay, of the outside world. After four years of death and destruction the old college was returning to life and there was a number of young unmarried dons, returned from their war-time avocations, dwelling in the college amongst us. It was not only the weekly tutorial—of which so much boast is now made—it was the constant, daily contact with dons, not only your own tutor, but dons of all kinds, theologians, scientists, philosophers, historians, who stopped you in the quad for a chat, who spoke at your debates, read papers at your literary societies, watched your games and invited you to meals. The daily company of really clever and very friendly men exercised upon my growing and expanding powers a truly educative influence. It has not meant nothing in my life that, when I was a young man at Merton, I once came upon F. H. Bradley in a corner of the garden standing stock still and unaware of any life around him, that I dined in the presence of Walter Raleigh, listened to his conversation, even perhaps took a drink or two too much in my excitement, that I took tea with prosy old Professor Wyld and heard him read a paper of monumental tedium to the Bodley Club, that I gasped at the grating scientific witticisms of E. W. B. Gill, lived on terms of almost intimate equality with Geoffrey Mure and Idris Deane Jones, tried, once or twice successfully, to get behind the somewhat prim, austere reserve of P. S. Allen, chatted and joked in incommunicable terms with the Rev. F. W. Green, and finally that I was the pupil of H. W. Garrod.

When I was up H. W. Garrod was still the Mods don and as such he was my tutor, and when he died some forty years later he was still my tutor—the only critic left whose good opinion I was resolute to obtain. Garrod was, I now think, a less renowned figure than his extraordinary talents deserved. Upon a deep foundation of classical learning he had erected an attractive superstructure of clever, if somewhat brittle, pavilions of ingenuity. He was alert and inventive, determined to find something new, to shake the elaborate fastnesses of what, in modern jargon, would be called the Establishment. He devoted perhaps more of his talents to this learned iconoclasm than would have seemed right to a maturer judgment. He was very clever and in Oxford this really means something. He was cleverer, it was generally thought, than the Balliol dons who taught him. He knew this, but in a sense he was humble about it; he believed that others were much cleverer than he. Why, I asked him many years later, why had P. S. Allen picked on him to complete, with Mrs. Allen, the comprehensive edition of Erasmus' letters. 'Why,' he said, 'why, because Allen thought I was roughly clever'—a superb understatement, about both his cleverness and his learning. As a Renaissance scholar he was in the first rank, as a classical scholar, where the competition was closer, he could have been if he had had a mind to. For sheer cleverness—of any problem, the immediate grab of understanding and the grasshopper leap to an ingenious solution—he was in his time unsurpassed. In controversial conversation, which not seldom he provoked, he would like Dr.

Johnson talk for victory and he would use any weapons that came to hand. If he required some authority—perhaps Johnson —to support his exaggerated point of view he would seize a copy of his works, search with counterfeit diligence for the appropriate page and invent what he was pretending to read with a skill of mimicry enough to deceive most antagonists. If he were not believed he would adopt an attitude of injured innocence and seem to take personal offence. Like Johnson too he would, if driven into a corner of weakness, seek to fight his way out with the aid of personal affronts. In literary controversy he could be equally pugnacious. His comments on bad scholarship, bad taste and above all dullness could be searing, while if he were attacked he would, like all dangerous animals, defend himself. It has been generally believed that A. E. Housman's attack upon his classical scholarship in the introduction to his Manilius Book V drove Garrod away from classical to English literature. Such a retreat would not, I think, have been in character, nor do the dates fit the theory. It is indeed more likely that an astringent lecture on *The Shropshire Lad* delivered by Garrod from the Oxford Chair of poetry stung Housman into his somewhat overdone critical aspersions.

During my years at Merton hardly a day passed without my spending some time in his company and the brilliance of his mind and of his conversation made a deep impression upon me. I was at once eager to develop my own critical judgment, to look at things as he did and to find phrases, not unworthy of his wit, in which to air my opinions. Many of us came under his spell and we caught not only his attitudes but his accents also. He spoke in a high quavering sing-song, his voice often fading away into little more than a whisper, and in conversations on mundane topics he often confused—perhaps on purpose— words and names. 'Do you like your tea hot or cold?' he would quaver out; and once in recounting to Dr. Bailey, a rather pompous Vice-Chancellor of Leeds University, a long story about Gilbert Murray in some game of telepathy he referred so continuously to 'poor old Bailey' instead of Murray that some of us, unable to repress our laughter, had to leave the room. Once I went with him to book rooms for a large party of us who were coming and going at different times to a favourite haunt of his at Abbotsbury and he so confused the poor woman by seeming to represent the bookings as cumulative that she cried in despair that her house had no more than six bedrooms and he was demanding eighteen. He could not understand how any confusion could have arisen and I had to overcome my laughter and put forward a practical plan. At Abbotsbury, at West Bay, in the Lakes and elsewhere I spent happy weeks with him. He was never an athletic figure, his legs perhaps a little short for a heavyish body, but he would on holiday walk his five miles or more. He did not himself play golf but he took delight in walking round with those of us who did, taunting and teasing us as he went. 'I can be very provocative, if I want to,' he would say, and it was quite true.

I think I learnt from Garrod that, if you want to be learned and clever, there is no need to be prosy and bookish about it. He was the most learned and the cleverest man I ever knew and he was also a king of nonsense, loving silly games and toys, inventing silly stories about people, spoiling his dogs, affecting ridiculous opinions, playing chess and bridge with light-hearted abandon. He would put forward an oracular statement, so apparently outrageous, that someone immediately challenged it, only to find himself beaten into surrender. 'I have an annoying habit of being right,' he would say, and that was true too. When matters of fact were not at stake he would still find reasons to support his strange pronouncements rather as Dr. Johnson found reasons for his astonishing remark—'If I had a seraglio, I would dress the women in linen'—so Garrod defended, what seemed at first an exhibition of prejudice—'Cooked cheese is a thing that should never be seen on a gentleman's table'—by arguing that as so many people disliked cooked cheese no gentleman would dream of offering it at a dinner party.

From Garrod I did not learn scholarship—which indeed I never acquired—but I did get a love of learning, a love of literature and a love of style. But above all, this man, separated from me by whole continents of academic skill and intellectual power, was my friend, generous, asking nothing in return, liking my company, it seemed, shyly affectionate, a limp handshake and some scarcely audible words of tender welcome or farewell, knowing so much more of the practical world in which I lived than most dons, ready with well-informed opinions, again like Johnson, on matters which, one would suppose, he had never considered, courtly in his manners to women, gentle, kind and tender-hearted, with such a strong moral sense—for all his anti-clerical views—that I took pains not to deserve his reproof. In my life—my family apart—his influence has been the most powerful and the best.

I was lucky enough to do exceedingly badly in the Schools— how badly and why it is not part of my intention to disclose, The luck of it consisted in this. My three years at Merton had, as I have tried to show, educated me in a broad sense and given me a love and respect for learning, but it had not provided me with an automatic passport to a safe career in one of the professions. I could not therefore regard myself as a highly educated product of this traditional system. I should have to show by personal achievement that I was better than my degree and, as I intended to be a schoolmaster, I should have to acquire a good deal more learning than I had so far. It was a useful lesson to learn, in early shame, that one's education is never completed. It was fortunate also that once, while I was an undergraduate, I tutored, in an Easter vacation, the son of Admiral Sir Percy Scott. The Admiral was a rash and controversial figure. I found him a little formidable but he used to grow mellow and, it must be admitted, a little confused after liberal indulgence in wine at dinner. He would then sometimes play bridge, invariably partnering himself with his daughter and me with his son. It was not very exciting but it was part of my duty. I did not complain because in his bibulous condition he frequently revoked and I felt no scruple about claiming the full penalty. At other times he would be anecdotal in a long-winded and roundabout way but there would be an occasional piece of worldly advice which took its place firmly in my consciousness. One such was—'Always learn the job of the chap above you. You never know when he will die or be dismissed and you must be ready to step into his shoes.' Perhaps that was the beginning of my preoccupation with the manners and modes of those on the levels above me.

Index

GEORGE MALLABY

SIR (HOWARD) GEORGE (CHARLES) MALLABY, whose career at the top of the British Civil Service spanned both Tory and Labor governments, was born in England in 1902 and was educated at Oxford University. For a number of years Sir George taught at several colleges in England and in South Africa. He was made a major in the British Army in 1941, rising to the rank of colonel in 1945. He served in the Military Secretariat of the War Cabinet during the war, and in 1946 received the U.S. Legion of Merit. From 1946 until 1948 he was Assistant Secretary of the Ministry of Defense and then, for two years, Secretary-General of the Brussels Treaty Defense Organisation. He was Under Secretary of the Cabinet Office from 1950 until 1954, when he became Secretary of the War Council of Ministers. From 1957 until 1959 he was High Commissioner for the United Kingdom in New Zealand. Sir George is now retired.